We're Traveling Light

Jocelyn Reichl

MOODY PRESS

CHICAGO

© 1976 by
THE MOODY BIBLE INSTITUTE
OF CHICAGO

Library of Congress Cataloging in Publication Data
Reichel, Jocelyn.
 We're traveling light.
  1. Aged—United States—Anecdotes, facetiae, satire, etc.
I. Title.
HQ1064.U6R4   301.43'5'0973   76-17305
ISBN 0-8024-9310-6

Printed in the United States of America

Contents

CHAPTER		PAGE
1.	Old Age Is Not for Sissies	7
2.	Ein, Zwei, Drei, Spiel!	13
3.	This One You Can Keep	18
4.	Moment of Truth	27
5.	A Man and His Dog	35
6.	So Much for Well-Laid Plans	44
7.	Roger	49
8.	The Years Draw Nigh	56
9.	Silas Marner, We Love You	59
10.	Thoughts on Moving Day	66
11.	Never Too Old	74
12.	The Doll House	83
13.	A Glorious Way to Go	90
14.	One Wife's Complaint	99
15.	Of Benches and Pews	109
16.	I Enjoyed You!	120

"This time we're traveling light," Everett warned.

1

Old Age Is Not for Sissies

I'M SO GLAD I can't take it with me when I shuffle off this mortal coil. I'm so relieved that there will be no luggage to pack, no effects to crate, no shopping bags to stuff. Because if it were so, I might never get to heaven; and if I did, I might never make it through the turnstyle—for I am an "eventuality" packer. I toss in boots and parkas for a trip to Phoenix and snakebite remedy and suntan oil for a weekend in New York City. My husband is so intimidated by the mountain of baggage that accompanies us on every trip that he feels it necessary to explain to the train conductors, the cabbies, and the airline clerks, "My wife doesn't want to get caught anywhere without the kitchen sink!"

I have tried to reform, believe me. Especially since my husband's third herniorraphy. On the eve of a trip, I cull, I weed, I determine to do without; but my insecurity invariably triumphs, and in go the longies and the seersucker suit, the vaporizer and the insect spray, the books and the Scrabble board.

"You call that a suitcase?" Everett asked me on one occasion, abandoning his own Spartan packing to discourage my enthusiasm. He poked around in the weekender that I had just dragged down from the closet shelf, sniffed in exasperation at the first aid kit and shook his head disgustedly at the family photograph album. He cued me again, "You call that a suitcase?"

"Well, what do you call it?" I countered, bristling and ready to defend my *semper paratus* philosophy right down to the three boxes of animal crackers for the grandchildren.

"Ha!" he snorted derisively. "It's not a *suit*case. It's an *in*-case!"

Overload was never a problem when the children were growing up. Granted, even on a short jaunt between Chicago and Milwaukee we managed to look like a royal entourage embarking on the first leg of an African safari; but since our four children did most of the toting, my idiosyncrasy was indulged. However, now that our offspring are long gone and far away, and my husband's patience, along with his strength, has diminished with the years, I try, more resolutely than ever before, to think small. I imagined I was succeeding until we made a trip to Quebec last year to spend Christmas with our oldest daughter's family.

The night before our departure Everett wagged a finger under my nose. "This time we are traveling light!" I nodded, mentally shifting clothing priorities—an extra dress for me, one less shirt for him.

"Look," he continued, taking hold of my wrists, "we have only four hands between the two of us. So that means no more than four bags—and that includes that miniature gladstone you call a purse."

I agreed with alacrity.

He was not convinced. "None of this tuck-it-under-your-arm, last-minute, can't-do-without-it merchandise," he warned. I was with him one hundred percent. We had three train connections to make in the tweny-five-hour journey, and no baggage accommodations along the way.

"We will take only what we can carry," I promised. That was not enough for Everett.

"In our hands," he amended.

It is amazing how much one can carry in one's hands. I say that only because I know it to be true. There we were, at 5:00 the next morning, sitting on a bench in Union Station, flushed, breathless, and a little dismayed; these two old-enough-to-know-better grandparents were barricaded behind enough baggage to warm the hearts of a couple of redcaps. But redcaps are extinct, I reminded myself. It was the two of us against the world.

I cast a covert glance at Everett. "How could I have done this to him?" I worried silently. His expression was bleak and full of self-reproach. "How could I have let you do this to me?" he telegraphed back.

A slippered, sweat-shirted janitor shuffled past us, pushing a longhandled broom. He looked at our luggage, at us, back at the luggage, and shook his head. I didn't blame him. At our feet were two pullman cases, a bulging garment bag, a train case, a rope-tied carton containing Christmas presents for the grandchildren, two pairs of skis and a cane. The cane was an emergency addition neither of us had anticipated.

I felt an apology might ameliorate the situation. "I'm sorry my heel gave out at the last minute," I said.

Everett didn't answer; he was eating his heart out watching a couple walk by with only two pieces of luggage between them.

"You know, you could go home and get the car. We can drive to Quebec in the same time the train trip takes."

"And what about your knees?" he reminded me, referring to the limited confines of our compact car and what we call my "migrating" arthritis, one of the pesty concomitants of middle age that I am learning to live "in spite of." Two or three hours on the road and I am beating a mad tattoo on the dashboard.

My burdened conscience drove me to make one more suggestion—a sacrificial one. "We can turn around and go home, call the whole trip off."

"Don't be foolish," he replied. "We reached the point of no return when I tipped the cab driver."

Relieved, I sat back and decided to think positively, to tally my blessings. I couldn't get past (a) by this time tomorrow we'll be six hours from our destination and (b) how good it would be to see the grandchildren.

I attempted to restore communications. "What are you thinking about?" I asked. Over thirty years of married life, and I have yet to learn that that is the most dead-end, unproductive question a wife can put to her husband.

"Nothing," Everett responded.

The sleepy janitor made a second pass in our vicinity, giving us another heavy-lidded once-over.

"Well, then, what do you suppose he's thinking?"

"He's probably of the opinion that whatever it is you broke, it serves you right, a woman your age skiing when you should be home."

"He's right," I interrupted, feeling my age and pains and thinking of the obstacle course we had to run in the next twenty-five hours. "I should be home, in bed, instead of gallivanting across the continent."

"You're suffering from 'packer's fatigue,' " Everett diagnosed. "Happens every trip. I'll take a walk over to the cafeteria and get us a snack. You'll feel better after you eat."

"Yes," I said, "comfort me with coke and a donut."

"I'll do more than that," he replied. "I'll give you some food for thought. Old age is not for sissies! Remember?"

I propped my aching foot on the train case and reflected on our motto. It certainly wasn't spiritual, not even the least bit inspirational. It was a statement of fact that we had picked up somewhere in our travels—a truism that often makes me wonder whatever became of "Grow old along with me; The best is yet to be."

"Old age is not for sissies" is an adage that Everett saves for moments of crisis and accomplishment; for example, when I took and passed my driving test at the age of forty-eight; when I learned to ride a ten-speed bike at forty-nine; when I took up cross-country skiing at fifty; and when I swam for the first time at fifty-one. Getting to Quebec by common carrier was no great accomplishment or challenge. I told him so when he returned with our snacks.

He thought it over, took a quick inventory, and pronounced: "Getting there, no. Intact, yes."

Well, we made it all right. There were helping hands along the way, including the Detroit native who warned us, "The cabbies will rob you!" and persuaded us that it would be wiser to take a bus to the train depot in Windsor. Actually, there were three buses—even change only on each—and it was the height of the rush hour. Being "ripped off" by a cab driver would have been a kinder fate.

In Toronto we had time between trains to revive our spirits with cheeseburgers, and by Montreal we had developed a sort of aplomb—we knew who would carry what. When we detrained at Ste. Foy and hugged our suddenly shy grandchildren, we were not only intact, we had added a box of cookies picked up somewhere along the way.

"Which proves," I said to Everett that night as we relaxed in our room in a two-hundred-year-old pension in Quebec's Old Town, "that where the spirit is willing, it doesn't make any difference what condition the flesh is in."

"That's just what I always say," he agreed. "Old age is not for sissies."

I sat in the deep window seat and looked out across the snow-covered park at the imposing Chateau Frontenac, looming like an enchanted castle, with its hundreds of illuminated dormers. I expected momentarily to see a cabriolet roll through the medieval archway and to hear the clop of hoofs on the cobblestone courtyard.

I was tired but impatient for tomorrow. Our daughter and son-in-law, on vacation from their French language studies at Laval University, would be taking us sight-seeing. They were missionaries with Wycliffe Bible Translators; their ultimate goal was to work with the Montagnais Indians in the northern part of the province of Quebec, transcribing the Scriptures into the native tongue. As "landed immigrants," Martha and Don were required to enroll in an intensive study of French. Four-year-old Phyllis and the two-year-old twins, Nathaniel and Benjamin, cared for during the day by a gracious French woman who spoke no English, were rapidly becoming bilingual.

I began to feel the cold probing my bones as I leaned against the window pane. A few feet from our hotel was the promenade that overlooked the Saint Lawrence River, and I could hear the faint sound of the whistles as the car ferries passed in mid-channel.

"Tomorrow we must take a ride on the ferry." I turned to Everett.

He didn't answer; he was sound asleep. Poor guy! It had been a strenuous trip. Come to think of it, I was exhausted too. Now, where did I—? In which suitcase? Or was it in the bottom of the garment bag that I had packed my pajamas? I sighed and began my search.

2
Ein, Zwei, Drei, Spiel!

ONCE UPON A TIME I chuckled at the cartoons which depict the bored husband accompanying his wife to the opera. In these humorous drawings it is always evident that the husband does not share his wife's enthusiasm for music. The "little man" is usually engaged in some devilish trick that will upset the equilibrium of a hefty Valkyrie or disconcert a helmeted Tristan in the middle of a rapturous duet with Isolde.

Now that I have "passed through the waters," I find the theme of these cartoons not at all funny. My sympathy no longer lies with the mischievous husband but with the soon-to-be-embarrassed wife. Let me explain.

Somewhere in my preengaged state I must have read a book, or perused an article, or dallied in a daydream that left me with the conviction that in order to achieve a happy marriage both partners must share the same interests, think the same thoughts, enjoy the same foods, and vote the same party. Later, therefore, when I became engaged, it was a matter of real concern to me when I discovered that my fiance did not share my taste in music. Everett had been brought up on "Casey Jones," "Big Rock Candy Mountain," and "Jatta," while I had been nurtured on symphonic concerts, piano and violin lessons, and daily exposure to an aunt who was a concert pianist. It was clear that the only musical selection on which Everett and I could reach any agreement was a certain tune from Lohengrin.

My job was cut out for me; the challenge was plain. Some women will marry a drunkard hoping to reform him. I would marry a musical illiterate and transform him into a Milton Cross. What I neglected to take into consideration was my fiance's origin—the mountains of Pennsylvania. Perhaps it's subsisting on a steady diet of pork shanks and sauerkraut, or growing up in the shadow of hex-marked barns, but whatever—a Dutchman of the Pennsylvania class is set in a stubborn mold.

I began—and ended—my first campaign on a Saturday night. Taking my brand-new husband to a Grant Park concert, I relied heavily on the cool lake breeze and the glow of the setting sun to provide a seductive atmosphere. When he held my hand snugly in his, my confidence soared. For thirty minutes he endured Sibelius and swatted mosquitoes with his free hand. Then, in the second movement of a Mendelssohn concerto, he bolted. And dragged me with him.

"That's it," he declared on the way home. "My first—and last—concert."

I was too unhappy to answer. For a brief moment I entertained visions of poetic justice. I would leave him and run away with a bald-headed bassoonist. On second thought, I would not leave him. I would stay and raise a string quartet! We declared a truce that August evening, but I resolved never to stop trying, and he promised to continue resisting.

My trying began with saving enough to buy a dilapidated old upright, and as the years went by, seeking out teachers who would give me a special rate, three children for the price of two, for example. Everett's resisting consisted mainly of never going to piano recitals and switching to the afternoon shift so that he wasn't home for practice sessions. There were times when I envied his independent spirit.

We maintained this stand-off position for years, and finally I gained a minor victory. Our children were to appear in a piano recital, and I was too ill to attend. Everett would have to go in my place. I commiserated with him, knowing he would be miserable. I could see him squirming through "Poupee Valsante;" sighing heavily during "The Happy Peasant;" walking out, perhaps, in the middle of "Marche Militaire." I assured him he would never have to go through such an ordeal again.

When he returned three hours later, looking none the worse for wear, he brushed aside my condolences with "It wasn't bad at all. In fact, I kind of enjoyed it."

This episode was not the beginning of the "Golden Age of Music" in our household, however; Everett had had what is known in medical circles as a "temporary remission." He returned to normal the next day. That is, he came home from work, turned off the stereo, and then kissed me.

Oh, there is some music that Everett will sit still for. But, as much as I love them, I can't spend the rest of my life listening only to George Beverly Shea and Helen Barth. I need a bit of Chopin and Mozart and Strauss interspersed.

"You are deprived," I sympathize. "You are missing so much that is lovely."

"Can I help it if I was born tone-deaf?" he defended himself.

And he was. It is most evident at church services in the congregational singing. Everett does not let his congenital handicap get in the way of his enthusiasm. In self-defense I hold my own hymnal and keep a safe distance. There was a time when, if he strayed too far off-key, I closed ranks and elbowed him in the ribs. He used to pay attention to my nudge and soft-pedal the

"You must be a professional!"

fortissimo somewhat. And then one night a few years ago, a visitor in our church, a woman in the pew immediately in front of ours, turned to him at the close of the service and said, "My, I enjoyed listening to you sing! You must be a professional."

We both swung around to see if she was speaking to someone behind us, but no, this positive thinker was addressing Everett.

"Do-gooder," I thought. "There'll be no living with him from now on."

And there hasn't been. He sings with even less inhibition and littler accuracy. The volume has increased and so has the cocksureness. He lives in hope that the miracle will recur, that one of these days another tone-deaf talent scout will turn to him and say, "What a voice! You must have had professional training!" He is even wondering aloud if all these years it hasn't been his wife who has the faulty perception, and not he.

Ah well, a happy married life is one of compromise. I continue to accompany Everett to church, and he has made it possible for me to have music whenever I want. He bought me a set of headphones to plug into my stereo! "There is one drawback, though," I told him. "I have to stay put once I'm plugged in."

He gave the problem considerable thought and came up with a solution. He wears the earphones—the plug in his pocket—and is insulated from the sound of music. Also from the sound of my voice. He is twice-blest, he says, ducking as I pretend to throw a Van Cliburn concerto in his direction.

3

This One You Can Keep

I DIDN'T CRY at my daughter's wedding. It wasn't for lack of a hanky that I held back the tears. My family had seen to it that I was provided with everything from absorbent tissues to something that resembled a miniature monogrammed tablecloth. They know well my propensity for tears. Anyone who watches the Waltons each week with a box of Kleenex in her lap could be expected to shed buckets at the nuptials of her firstborn.

But I didn't. I was too busy repressing a grin. Too jubilant to shed a tear. Doesn't the Bible say that there is a time for everything? A time to weep and a time to laugh? To mourn and to dance? Well, Martha's wedding day was no time for weeping or wailing. It was a time to kick up one's heels!

Why was I so indecently exuberant? Had I been in despair that no one would pop the question? Hardly. Martha takes after the women in my husband's family. She's a Janet Lynn, a Dresden figurine of a girl, who never has to open a door or stand on a crowded bus or wait her turn in line.

No, we never worried about Martha's being overlooked. What did concern us was the possibility that Martha might overlook Mr. Right. You see, our young daughter suffered from both a total lack of discrimination and an inordinate compassion for the weak and helpless—excellent qualifications for the mission field or a life of social service but not for the selecting of one's life companion.

We had been aware of her handicap for a long time. Before Martha was five years old, she was in the habit, as it were, of being followed home by stray dogs and undernourished kittens. When she was only seven, her bedroom, which I vainly attempted to keep beruffled and feminine, had become an aviary filled with orphaned sparrows and crippled robins.

We sent her to camp when she was eight years old, and she returned home with sun-bleached tresses, a peeling nose, and a surprise—a collection of Mason jars with perforated lids, containing specimens from an exciting new world—amphibia.

She hammered open her piggy bank at the age of nine to buy a fullgrown garter snake from a classmate with a prejudiced parent—more prejudiced than I, apparently.

By the time she was ten, Martha's reputation had spread to such proportions that her Dad considered building a night depository on our rear porch. All the family was in favor and voted "aye," with one exception. I was still trembling from an encounter with our daughter's latest boarder, a female opossum with a pouch full of young and a vicious snarl.

"She won't hurt you, Mom," Martha insisted, coaxing the protesting creature back into her cage, a temporary shelter until we could take her back to the woods from which she had strayed. Martha and her brother had rescued the animal from some juvenile tormentors.

"We have no one to blame but ourselves," Everett admitted, the day our daughter returned from a school picnic with a moribund bat in her lunchbox. "If we don't start discouraging her, we'll wake up some morning to find ourselves dead of rabies or tularemia."

It was our fault, all right. I suppose it began with my determination that none of our children would grow up with the same irrational fears about animals that I had acquired. Since the children weren't liable to meet anything but the usual cats, dogs, and city birds in our northwest side neighborhood, I encouraged importation and for the most part was able to hide my revulsion as the steady stream of exotic and under-the-rock creatures came to share our bed and board.

There was Jerry the white rat, for example. He may have been a beauty, as the whole family insisted, but I could not forgive him his tail. Martha soon learned that Mommy did not appreciate having him dumped into her lap as a surprise nor smuggled under the bed clothes as a foot warmer and that there wasn't anything their Uncle Pete would like more for a birthday present than Jerry the rat.

The hamsters were a consolation present to make up for the loss of the rat. They were irresistible; they kept us awake all night; and after they had lived out their normal in-captivity life span (which means they eventually disappeared into the woodwork), they were not replaced. Unless the white mouse that Everett brought home from work could be called a replacement.

Everett had rescued the mouse, an escapee from a Railway Express shipment, on the eve of our vacation trip east. We would be traveling by train, and the mouse presented a problem. Martha pleaded, promised, and prevailed. Her dad sat up half the night fashioning a traveling cage out of a wooden cheese box. Doing what came naturally, the mouse began gnawing at his cell just outside of Gary, Indiana, and poked his whiskered head through the tiny aperture as we pulled into Detroit. Martha caught him before he could trigger a stampede in the passenger coach.

It was in Philadelphia that our five-year-old got her first glimpse of genuine hysteria. She walked into our hostess's living

"Take it away! Oh, please take it away!"

room, mouse in hand, eager to introduce her pet to the gathering. A visiting relative, a plump matron about fifty, took one look at the mouse and lost all control. Martha stood there, running her pet from one hand to the other, wondering what had gotten into the funny lady, who kept screaming from her unsteady perch on the sofa, "Take it away! Oh, please take it away!"

I shared Martha's amazement. Antipathy towards some animals I can readily understand, but how a grown woman could give way to such frenetic behavior, merely at the sight of a mouse—and a white mouse, at that—was beyond my comprehension.

That is, it was until four years later when I was "tabled" by a garter snake. Martha, whose snake it was, Tom, and Debby were in school. Two-year-old Joanna, clad only in diapers that warm morning, was playing contentedly on the floor when the creaking of the dining room table attracted her attention. She looked up from the block tower she was constructing. There sat her mother, atop the table, waving her arms and trying to speak. Joanna was not so much alarmed as she was curious at the strange perspective.

"Whatamatta?" she lisped.

I pointed to the corner of the room where Martha's twenty-inch serpent was awkwardly propelling itself across the waxed linoleum.

"Uh-huh," she acknowledged. " 'nake." And she resumed her construction work.

I took a measure of courage from her unconcern and assessed the situation. I could sit on the table until noon when the children came home for lunch, but that was three hours away. In the meantime the telephone might ring, a neighbor might knock, and Joanna would certainly need some attention. Besides, I had no assurance that the snake, now trying unsuccessfully to climb the wall, would not turn next to the ornately carved table leg and find it easier to scale. I did the most heroic thing I could, under the circumstances.

"Joanna," I croaked. "Pick up the snake and put him back into his cage." I tried for a cool, calm delivery—an I'd-do-it-myself-sweetheart-if-I-weren't-so-busy-holding-down-the-table tone of voice. It worked.

"Pick up da 'nake? OK," she said. She knocked down her tower, padded barefoot across the room, and after a brief struggle held the writhing creature tenderly and affectionately against her bare chest, looking for all the world like the infant Hercules. Standing as tall as she could, she strained and grunted and finally was able to drop him into his windowsill terrarium.

"Mommy, you can come down now," she said sympathetically.

That was in June. In July Martha and the snake left for Camp Awana with instructions that only one of them was to return. She agreed with alacrity. I should have been suspicious; the alacrity in this kind of situation was abnormal. Three weeks later when she returned home, we discovered that, yes, she had left the snake in a Wisconsin bog, but she had eased the wrench of the separation by bringing home several additions to her frog and toad collection. I groaned, thinking of the neighbors. Already they were talking about our family's foraging around garbage cans. How does one communicate across the backyard fence that one's husband and children are prowling the alleys in order to provide dinner for a dozen amphibians?

Everett, of whom it can never be said that he wouldn't even hurt a fly, taught the children the fine art of fly-catching: the cupped palm, the slow approach from the front, and then the surprise rush, followed by the deft removal of a wing and the popping into the milk bottle.

Every time I protested—and I protested every time—he would

23

reply, "Well, it's that or remove the window screens and let the flies come to us." The other alternative never occurred to us: get rid of the fly-eaters.

Yes, on the animal issue we leaned over backward; we wanted the children to experience life to the fullest. We couldn't get out into the countryside, so we encouraged the children to bring the country into our city apartment. I had another motive. I wanted to encourage the faculty of wonder in our youngsters, to get across the message that a mouse or guinea pig or parakeet or snake is "miracle enough to stagger sextillions of infidels."

While all four of the children loved animals, it was Martha whose single-minded dedication worried me. I feared her growing up into a legend of eccentricity—a musty recluse, known to the neighborhood as "The Cat Lady of Irving Park."

"Don't worry," Everett advised. "One of these days she'll discover that boys are a whole lot more interesting than animals, and your troubles will be over."

"Do you really think so?" I grasped eagerly at the prospect.

The day did come, even as he had prophesied. When Martha trembled on the brink of sixteen, sure enough, she discovered the other sex. With what relief we watched as she dispassionately disposed of cages, aquaria, flea powder, and mange medicine! But our relief was premature. True, she may have switched her allegiance from zoology to anthropology, but she had not lost her propensity for rescue and salvage operations.

No potentially rabid bat or tularemic rabbit had ever frightened us as much as her bizarre succession of swains—all of them in desperate need of someone to love them, to understand them, to shelter them from life's wintry blasts. Each time Martha introduced us to another teenage derelict, it was as though she were saying, as in days of yore, "Look what I found! May I keep it?"

This time around we were not permissive; we were tactlessly antagonistic. We could not pretend we were pleased with Tom, the masochist; or Dick, the reformatory alumnus; or Harry, a sullen Heathcliff. How we longed for the good old days when our arguments had centered around such impersonal issues as mouse odors and escaping opossums!

We prayed, of course. We had long, emotional confabs. When words failed, we sent intrafamily notes to each other. Somehow, we survived the ordeal; and when Martha left for college at the age of nineteen, she was unattached, and we were still friends. And I had aged ten years in three.

I was a little uneasy about Martha's being four hundred miles away from our protective custody. At it turned out, I needn't have been. Working twenty to thirty hours a week in addition to carrying a full academic load, she had little time for socializing.

"Besides," she wrote, out of a surprising new fastidiousness, "I don't like what I see." That was in her sophomore year, and I figured she had plenty of time left for looking around.

But when she was in her junior year, I began to fret. "What kind of college is that, anyway? She's not engaged yet."

When she was graduated the following year with a degree in art and anthropology and no matrimonial prospects, I wondered if we hadn't been too negative about her beaus, if maybe we had encouraged her to be so idealistic that nobody was good enough for her.

Martha did not share my concern. When she entrained for Seattle the day after commencement to enroll in a summer linguistic course at the University of Washington, she was confident that the Lord had someone waiting there for her.

She was right. Before many days had passed, we received a letter in which she rapturously exclaimed, "I'm in love!" and triumphantly declared, "At last I've found someone you'll like!"; and added as a clincher, "You'll have to. He's just like Dad!"

I didn't cry at Martha's wedding. I suppose I let everyone down—my family, the guests, and tradition. I couldn't help it. I sat there smiling broadly and remembering.

I was recalling a pig-tailed tomboy who tenderly loved all of God's helpless creatures, bringing them home with her and asking each time, "May I keep this one?" I was remembering, too, a teenage charmer who had looked upon each boyfried as a rehabilitation project needing her particular brand of solicitude. And I was comforted and elated by the knowledge that this time Martha had reached out—not down—for love.

The organist had just finished the Crimond version of the Twenty-third Psalm; and Martha, in a simple white frock and short veil, walked slowly down the aisle on her father's arm. For a brief second her eyes left Don's and met mine. She was smiling, too. This time she hadn't had to ask. She knew that we liked what she had found, that this one she could keep.

4
Moment of Truth

EVERETT'S MOMENT OF TRUTH was late in arriving. A man as well preserved as he is, who still takes the steps two at a time, is not ready to recognize the "bending sickle" even if it is poised right over his graying head. I'm afraid Everett had been lulled into a false sense of security by the frequent rave notices of those who refused to believe he antedates the airplane. I grant he is growing old gracefully, and that after a shave and a haircut and a good night's sleep he could fool even a carnival huckster whose business it is to guess weights and ages. His youthful appearance has deceived a good many people, including himself.

"I owe it all to eggs," he confides when his friends inquire about his abundance of energy and his *joi de vivre*. He does consume eggs at an alarming rate, averaging about three a day; and I have known days when that number has shot up to seven or eight. Cholesterol holds no terrors for him. At this writing, my calculations show that he has eaten a grand total of 48,180 eggs over the years; and during each of those years he has exhausted about three and a quarter hens—not ordinary hens, mind you, but jumbo layers.

Personally, I don't take much stock in the rejuvenating power of eggs, since I eat a fair share myself; and even after a facial and a hairdo and a good night's sleep, I not only look my age but quite often a little bit more.

No, I really can't go along with Everett's fruit-of-the-chicken theory. I'm convinced that his secret lies in his state of mind; he is a nonworrier. He was born to be content in whatsoever situation he found himself, and he has remained true to his calling. There were a lot of lessons he had to learn when he became a Christian, but contentment was not one of them. He calls himself a Calvinist; I call him an acquiescent believer. Be that as it may, one of the thousand and one things he has never fretted about is the problem of growing old. He was so indifferent to the "inevitable specter" that he didn't recognize its presence even when *Modern Maturity Magazine* appeared on the coffee table cheek by jowl with *National Geographic* and *Eternity*.

He seemed to possess a psychological shortsightedness that prevented his reading the signposts along the way. For example, he could never remember the name of the club that he belonged to, a group of local citizens who met every month in the town of Ellison Bay. There was a mental block, no doubt about it, that made it impossible for him to recall the name of that particular organization. A typical conversation would go something like this:

HE   We're having an auction sale at the next meeting.
SHE *(frankly puzzled):* Who is?
HE   *(after deep thought):* The people who meet at the schoolhouse.
SHE *(pretending innocence):* What people?
HE   *(beginning to fidget):* You know, the Tuesday afternoon group.
SHE *(pursuing relentlessly):* How would *I* know. I'm in Chicago on Tuesdays.
HE   *(getting hot under the collar):* It's the group I joined last October.

LA BELLE DAME SANS MERCI: You've joined so many organizations, I can't keep track.
HE (*pleading*): You know I can't remember the name. It's the old people.
SHE (*helpfully*): You mean the Senior Citizens Club, don't you?
HE (*sighing gratefully*): Yes, that's it. The Senior Citizens.

There were other myopic indications along the way. He referred to a neighbor whom I had yet to meet as the "little old lady who lives down the road." She turned out to be a charming, intellectual, beautifully-groomed woman—silver-haired, true—but at least ten years Everett's junior.

"Well, she looks like somebody's grandmother," he insisted, defending his description.

Even the mutilations of the scythe Everett was able to ignore. "At your age—" the optician commiserated, and Everett came home with his first pair of bifocals.

"Whaddya know," he said that afternoon from behind the pages of the *Daily News*, "They've started using a different type. The print's larger and darker. I wouldn't have had to get these stupid glasses after all." He was dead serious.

The partial plate that followed soon after the bifocals was not due to aging, Everett hastened to explain. Years before, one of our children had playfully whipped back her head while sitting on his lap, cracking his front teeth above the gum line.

"Could happen to anyone," he reassured the family and himself.

Later, Everett claimed it was the hardware that anchored the partial that contributed to the total breakdown. When the dentist said, "At your age, you've got to expect—", Everett cut him off with a choking sound, which was all he could manage around the dentist's knuckles, but which meant, "I'm too young to go the whole route, Doc."

His first bursitis attack sent Everett to the family physician with the story that he must have twisted his shoulder while lifting a heavy box at work. Plunging the needle into Everett's left deltoid, the doctor said, "Well, you know, at your age—" but he was speaking in the vicinity of my husband's left ear, which hasn't been functioning too well for the past few years, and so the prognosis didn't register.

The eroding hairline was such a gradual change that it was almost unnoticeable; only comparison with the early family snapshots revealed the difference that time had wrought. Everett took care of that problem by stowing the daguerrotypes on an inaccessible closet shelf.

If the doctor, dentist, and mirror could not convince him, who or what could, I wondered. Not that I was out to cramp Everett's style, mind you. I just wanted to stop him from pushing neighbors' cars out of ditches, rescuing cats from trees, and volunteering himself into three-legged races at church picnics, that's all. I wanted him to slow down to a safe speed and conserve his energy before it ran out on him. Also, I was tired of my role of backseat driver, both in and out of the car; and I am certain he was just as weary of hearing "Take it easy," "Slow down," "Remember your shoulder," "You're not getting any younger," "Wear something warmer," et cetera—loving admonitions that went unheeded because Everett was confident they did not apply to him.

His quick and nimble footwork enabled him to sidestep the old-age issue for a long while, but then one day when his guard was down it hit him. His moment of truth occurred, as most revelations do, in a very ordinary and incongruous setting. For him it was the A & W lunchroom in Two Rivers. We had ordered our usual Momma- and Poppa-burgers; and while we waited, we discussed the witty signs posted on the walls.

When you have been married as many years as we have, you become grateful for any conversational assists you can get. Long silences are not necessarily strained; on the contrary, they are often quite comfortable; but in a public place you want to keep up the fiction that, old and married though you may be, you still find each other's company exciting and the dialogue fresh and sparkling—so much so, that the waitress approaching to take your order is an interruption and not a relief. Those are my sentiments. Everett would just as soon sit quietly and listen to his stomach growl.

I digress; but I do it consciously, in order to explain to those who haven't yet reached the stage of interminable companionable silences what desperate remedies we wives will take to keep up appearances. I read about a woman in my predicament—insecure and married to a taciturn male—who, when the conversation lagged, resorted to reciting nursery rhymes over the restaurant table. She would lean forward, eyes sparkling, face animated, as though she were about to impart some intimate and exciting confidence.

"Did you know that Mary had a little lamb?" she would ask breathlessly.

"Is that so?" her husband responded, trying to enter into the spirit of the game.

"Yes," she would aspirate excitedly, "and its fleece was white as snow!"

Continuing to cooperate, her mate would ask, "Whatever happened to that lamb?"

"Well" was her response, accompanied by a shrug of the shoulders, "everywhere that Mary went, the lamb was sure to go."

He was responding in his best falsetto, "What, lost their mittens? Those naughty kittens!" when the waitress slipped up on us.

"And what was Mary's itinerary?" he asked as though he really cared.

"It followed her to school one day—"

He raised his eyebrows disapprovingly and interrupted, "Wasn't that against the rules?"

"Oh, yes," she admitted. "But it made the children laugh and play to see a lamb at school."

Nobody at the surrounding tables would ever have guessed that they were an old married couple from the looks of them, this writer insisted. I thought it was worth a try. The waitress slipped up on us while Everett was responding in his best falsetto, "What? Lost their mittens? Those naughty kittens!"

We are back to long, comfortable silences and motto reading.

That's what we were doing the day that the scales fell from Everett's eyes, reading the writings on the wall. I pointed out a plaque that read, LORD, GIVE ME PATIENCE, SOON. Everett liked the one which read, DON'T CRITICIZE THE COFFEE. YOU MAY BE OLD AND WEAK YOURSELF SOMEDAY. We both laughed over PLEASE DON'T SHOOT THE CHEF. HE'S DOING THE BEST HE CAN!

We were halfway through our meal when Everett spotted another sign on the wall, an announcement posted behind the cash register. He began to read it aloud:

SENIOR CITIZENS
10% Discount
Monday through Friday
1-4 p.m.

"That's nice," he approved. "That's a nice thing for them to do," he added with only a faint trace of condescension. He bit into his sandwich then abruptly stopped, mouth open, eyes bulging, Adam's apple working. I was alarmed. The words "cafe coronary" sprang to mind. Before I could rush to his aid, he managed a whisper.

"That means me," he choked.

I patted his hand, relieved and sympathetic. "I know, Everett. I know."

We ate the rest of our meal in silence. The intensity of his preoccupation was evidenced by the fact that he neglected to filch half my French fries, and he refused a third cup of coffee. He was busy wrestling with the revelation. As we rose to leave, I was encouraged by the conspiratorial grin he gave me.

"Well?" I asked.

"I've decided," he winked, "that if you don't tell them, neither will I."

No matter that he kept his secret from the pretty young waitresses at the A & W—his moment of truth had arrived; he had recognized it; and things would never be quite the same again. Everett soon took to wearing bedroom slippers all day long, out in the barn, shopping, gardening, until a daughter told me how to remedy the situation. Hide the slippers. Then he began shaving only on alternate days. I considered hiding the razor since a beard seemed preferable to stubble. After further consideration, I decided to let him have that round, especially since he had given in on one of my major demands, retiring as neighborhood troubleshooter. Now, when the neighbors spin their wheels in the wet snow, he watches from the warmth and security of the house, hidden from sight behind the living room curtains, chuckling uncharitably.

And, oh yes, the mental block has disappeared. He remembers, without my prompting, that it's the Senior Citizens that meet on the second Tuesday of the month. And that he is a member, not a mascot.

5

A Man and His Dog

WHEN I WALKED into the house one day with a pound and a half of Chihuahua in my purse, Everett demanded, "What have you got there?"

"It's a panacea," I hedged. "You work nights. I work days. I get lonesome."

"That's a poor excuse," he snorted.

"I don't think I need much of an excuse," I sniffed, huffily on the defensive.

"For a dog," he amended. "That's a poor excuse for a dog."

"She'll grow," I promised. "She's only six weeks old."

"She'll get sucked up into the vacuum cleaner first," he predicted. "What kind of dog is she supposed to be?"

"She's supposed to be—I mean, she is a long-haired Chihuahua. We'll get her papers in a few days."

"And the long hair? When will that arrive?"

"They told me she'll get her first full coat in about six months."

"Well, until then you'd better buy her a wig. She's shivering."

I couldn't blame Everett for his lack of enthusiasm. A man has dreams about the kind of dog he would like to own. He imagines himself donning a rugged mackintosh on a blustery October evening and loping ankle-deep in fallen leaves with a well-trained airedale at his heels, or clad in thick brogans and country corduroys striding over hill and dale with a brace of red setters frolicking on ahead, or driving down the crowded expressway in a station wagon with a Great Dane drooling over his leather-patched tweeds. Dreams like those die hard. There is no way a man can snap a leash onto twenty-four ounces of quaking dogflesh and manage to stride with dignity down the boulevard. But I had thoroughly researched the pet possibilities—a computor couldn't have been more objective—and for folks of our age, teetering on doddering; and our life-style, sedentary with frequent aberrations; and our living accommodations, rented city apartment on weekdays, mobile home in the country on weekends, a portable pup was indicated.

My one miscalculation had been not consulting Everett first, but that's my usual m.o., to confront him with the *fait accompli* and let the chips fall where they may. I have learned that my husband, who is able to argue all joy out of a proposal, bows gracefully to the inevitable, eventually.

The next morning at breakfast I attempted to get him involved. "The dog has to have a name," I reminded him.

He thought for a moment. "I have a suggestion," he said. "When I was a boy on the farm in Harrison Valley—"

"Here it comes," I groaned.

"—my brother and I had a pair of collie pups," he went on, ignoring my interruption. "Rudy called his You Know."

"And you named yours Guess," I supplied.

"That's right. And every time somebody would ask us what their names were, we'd tell them—" He couldn't finish; he was doubled over in laughter at the recollection. No matter how often he told that story—and he told it very often—it would break him up.

I waited for him to recover, and then I continued, "It should be a Spanish name. After all, she is of Mexican origin."

"That's no problem. How about Tortilla? Enchilada? Tostados? Taco? he suggested, drawing upon his one excursion to an ethnic restaurant. "Don't laugh," he advised. "How much Spanish do you know?"

"Poquito," I admitted. "Which translated means 'not very much,' I think.

"Poquito," he said, trying it out. "Since she certainly isn't very much of anything herself, it ought to fit her perfectly."

Poquito, knowing no more about Spanish grammar than we did and aiming only to please, took to her name immediately. She also responded to such endearments as "Babydoll," "Sweetiepie," "Poochie," "good girl," and a casual glance in her general direction. Everett persisted in calling her "Hey, you!" and often just plain "dog," either of which sent her into ecstatic convulsions—to which he was impervious, I should add. To him she was a bit of ornamental fluff, a lady's lap dog. He would try to avoid inadvertently stepping on her or closing a door on her tail, but I was not to expect any more than that.

"You bought her," he reminded me the day I asked him if he would take her in for her shots. "You paid for her with your own egg money. So you walk her, and you take her to the vet. She's your dog."

He carefully avoided looking at Poquito while he issued the ultimatum. She was flopped across his instep, wagging her little tail furiously, eyes brimming over with liquid love.

"I can't, Everett. I can't bear to see the vet stick the needle into her. I couldn't stand it with the *other* children either. Remember?" Fortunately, he didn't notice my slip.

He relented. "All right, just this once," he warned, tucking her under his arm and slipping out of the house after dark.

I hadn't anticipated it; but when they returned, I noticed a new relationship had sprung up between them—a camaraderie from which I was excluded. I suppose it was because they had shared a painful experience: she had been inoculated, he had paid the bill. Everett was not admitting a thing, however. He merely dumped her unceremoniously into my lap and retreated behind the evening paper.

A few days later, arriving home from work, I discovered that Everett had hung a tiny stuffed bear from the floor lamp for Poquito to bat and wrestle. He dismissed appreciation with "She was bored, always pestering to get up into my lap."

The following week I walked into the house to find that a lookout platform had been installed on the living room windowsill so that Pokey could sun herself and bark at canine passersby. A padded ramp provided easy access. Ignoring the facts that it didn't do much for the decor and that it ended under the foot pedals of the piano, I praised the contraption.

"I can't keep getting up every time that mutt wants to look out the window," was his rationalization.

When spring arrived and we got our bicycles out of the barn for a trial run, it was Everett who decided that, if we didn't take Poquito along, I'd probably worry all the time we were away. He fastened a harness to a carrying basket and secured it to the handlebars of his bicycle. "She'll be safer with me," he explained, referring to my inability to get on or off a bike without incident.

Poquito, after a few minutes of anxiety, got into the spirit of the sport. Leaning into the wind, eyes squinted almost shut, ears folded back, she suggested a streamlined radiator ornament. It was on that maiden trip, however, that we discovered she was not merely decorative; she became a working member of the crew.

Heretofore, we had had to arm ourselves with rocks, spray guns, aerosol whistles, and water pistols loaded with soapy water in order to repel vicious, cycle-chasing dogs. None of these

I pedaled furiously lest the bloodthirsty hounds turn on me in their frustration.

weapons was really effective. But now, with Pokey in the vanguard, we were safe. Farm dogs, leaping from ambush and aiming for our ankles or calves, were suddenly distracted by Pokey's hysterical barking. They continued to pursue us, but they were no longer interested in hamstringing; they were infuriated by the taunting insults, the catch-me-if-you-cans emanating from our Mexican spitfire.

I don't know who enjoyed those encounters more—Poquito or Everett. Certainly not I, pumping furiously to keep up, lest the blood-thirsty hounds, unable to gain on their quarry, turn on me in their frustration.

It must have been Poquito's fierce Aztecan heart that was breaking down the last barriers of Everett's resistance, because when I suggested we leave her with one of the children while we took a trip to Arizona, he seemed a little put out. "There's no need," he said. "She's a good traveler." I wouldn't have been surprised by this time if he had added, "Besides, I want to show her the West. She's never seen it."

He built her a cushioned car seat and mounted it between us so that she had a clear view of Highway 66 all the way there, and I had a clear view of Everett only at gas and meal stops.

He had been right about her, though. She was an ideal traveling companion, thriving on doggybag meals and thrilled as a kid with each new motel room. Something we hadn't counted on was her social contribution. People found her so irresistible that we never lacked for company. Hardly anyone could pass by without asking about her lineage. Tourists paused in their inspection of the Grand Canyon to comment, "What a beautiful dog! What kind is she anyway?" I rarely got a chance to tell them; Everett was right there to take full credit.

The first few times he opted for accuracy. "She's a long-haired Chihuahua." Almost invariably the response was a skeptical

"Izzatso? Never heard of it." Which meant that Everett had to prove his veracity and her purity by explaining that there is indeed such a breed and that in fact the AKC had our pup on file. It was a lot of trouble after the first twenty or thirty encounters. He decided finally that people would rather believe a lie—or at least hear one—and so he began to dream up weird answers. To the query "What kind of dog is that?" Everett, looking the interrogator in the eye, would reply, "She's a miniature Great Dane." The response was usually an indulgent laugh, which was preferable to a genealogical discussion.

Others would tell us, "She looks just like a young fox. What kind of dog is she? Oh, she's not a dog? She's a domesticated fox? Whaddya know!" they'd marvel, going along with the gag. Everett also tried shrunken sheltie, and dwarf caribou, dehorned, of course.

It was on that trip West that Everett learned that Poquito was a drawing card especially attractive to ladies, young and old. Consequently he exercised her to a frazzle.

Pokey had been with us for five years when she had her accident, a fall from a porch causing serious damage to a knee. She underwent surgery and was subsequently hospitalized for eleven days. We anguished a little knowing how miserable she must be, and we plagued the vet daily with calls about her condition. At the same time we noticed a sense of liberation, not unlike the first months after our last child left the nest. Everett and I rediscovered each other; we began to communicate tete-a-tete instead of via Poquito. ("Pokey, what's Mother fixing for dinner?" or "Pokey, go tell Dad we'd like to go out for a drive.") We found that we were sitting closer together on the sofa now that we didn't have to leave room for the dog. We held hands.

"Where have you been for the last few years?" Everett teased while we were watching TV on one of our nights alone.

"Just a dog's length away," I replied.

"Do you mean Pokey's been coming between us?"

"You'd better believe it! Every time you felt affectionate, you'd cuddle Poquito."

"Instead of you!" he said wonderingly.

"Instead of me," I agreed.

"We were such a happy threesome, I thought."

"More like a triangle," I countered.

"Why didn't you tell me I was neglecting you?" he demanded.

"I thought it was just that I was getting old and repulsive," I sighed.

"Nonsense," he reassured me. "From now on things will be different. We'll keep a proper perspective. We'll put Poquito to bed at an earlier hour. We'll hire a baby-sitter and go out more often."

The honeymoon and Everett's promises lasted until the day we drove to Green Bay to pick up our convalescent. She was emaciated and had a racking cough. Her shaved, stitch-puckered leg stuck out grotesquely from her body. I steeled myself. "A proper perspective," Everett had said. She was, after all, only a dog.

I started for the right side of the car, when Everett stopped me and snatched the ailing dog from my arms. "You drive," he ordered. "I'll hold the poor little thing."

That night I got out of bed around midnight to check on the patient. I had installed her in her cage a couple of hours earlier, wrapping her in a flannel blanket and laying her on top of my new heating pad. She was not there; the cage was empty and open. She and Everett were curled up sound asleep on the sofa. As I bent over them, Pokey opened one eye and closed it again. A slow wink.

"You little vixen!" I whispered, tucking the cover more securely around the two of them.

"Ah well," I philosophized later in my lonely room. "I asked for it." How had Bernard, that wise and holy monk, phrased it? "Qui me amat, amat et canum meum."*

---

*"Who loves me, let him love my dog also."

6

So Much for Well-Laid Plans

PHYLLIS WAS COMING and I was beside myself with joy. The cupboard was stocked with boxes of animal cookies and carmel corn; the freezer with three different flavors of ice cream; the refrigerator with chocolate milk and white, and a shelf of fruit juices and punch. The candy dishes were filled and placed at eye level—hers, that is; and there were strawberry tarts and sugar cones from Beil's Bakery.

"You will kill her with kindness," Everett warned.

"Oh, but I want her to remember this visit," I protested.

"Don't worry. She will. She's probably never in her young life seen a stomach pump or a dentist."

"You think I'm overdoing it?"

"Maybe just a little," he suggested. "I don't think she will be able to handle Christmas, Easter, and her birthday all rolled up into one."

"I want to make a good impression. I want her to like me."

"Listen, she liked you in San Diego when she was only a baby. She liked you last summer when she was only two. What makes you think she will suddenly dislike you at three?"

"She will be more discerning," I sighed. "She will recognize that I am a rank amateur next to her California grandmother."

"So that's why you're trying harder—you think you're second best? Take my advice and relax. You don't see me wearing myself to a frazzle trying to compete with her California grandpa, do you?"

"You're right," I conceded. "As usual, I'm pushing too hard." Everett started out the door.

"Where are you going?" I asked. "You promised to help with the dishes."

"Out to the barn. I've got to get Phyllis's bicycle seat finished; and the dining room furniture for the doll house needs a second coat of varnish."

"Well, don't work yourself to a frazzle out there," I admonished drily.

I had begun my countdown about three weeks before, and now Phyllis was due to arrive the next day. In my enthusiastic planning I occasionally lost sight of the fact that she was going to be accompanied by her parents and infant twin brothers. I would be delighted, naturally, to see our daughter and son-in-law; and I was sure the identical twins would be fascinating and a joy to behold, but it was Phyllis for whom the strategy had been laid out.

I went to the closet to peek at the dress I had made for her; it was finished, all but the hem. Phyllis was such a little thing. How tall has she grown? I wondered. In my memory, she had held still. I rearranged the furniture in the doll house—a red, white and green Victorian mansion that Everett had completed since her last visit. Would she understand that it was still in the making, that it was only a promise as yet? I straightened the nursery rhyme and story books on the bedside table. Hans Christian Andersen! Whatever had possessed me? The stories would frighten her out of her wits. I removed that particular book and put it on a closet shelf.

Admittedly, I was anxious. It wasn't as though Phyllis lived next door or even in the same town and was running in and out the back door, on chummy terms with my cookie jar. We had seen our first granddaughter only twice, and to her we were but a legend. I wanted this visit to be a memorable one for her; I wanted her to take away enough vivid and lasting impressions to carry over until Christmas when we hoped to join her in Quebec.

I had made a list of activities that I thought might be exciting "firsts" for her—one for each day of the week that she would be with us. I planned toothsome dishes that I thought would be especially appealing. I shampooed and brushed Poquito as though she were going into the show ring, and I bought her a new collar.

"Phyllis is coming!" I sang to the bewildered pup as I whirled her around the living room.

They arrived in their VW camper the next afternoon, the parents weary, the boys hungry, and Phyllis shy. After a night's sleep, she trusted me enough to accompany me on a prebreakfast walk to a neighboring farm where she fed lumps of sugar to a spindle-legged colt. We spent the warm evening on a rocky beach tossing stones into the water, and she was persuaded to leave only by the promise that we would return the next night to finish the job.

Another day I took her to a nearby stable for her first pony ride. She was more impressed with the young boy who led her steed, but that's the way with a maid.

The waves were rough the day we went to Newport Beach, but she was not disappointed, content to build castles and canals in the sand.

I held her up high so she could feed soda pop to a black bear at the local outdoor zoo, and she stood breathlessly still while a young buck ate from her hand at a deer preserve.

She licked frosting bowls and patted her own meat loaf into

We fed lumps of sugar to a spindle-legged colt.

its doll-sized pan, stirred the jello and sliced the bananas, and dropped tidbits to Poquito.

She froze while the ruby-throated hummingbird paused on his way to the feeder to inspect the red ribbon I had tied in her hair. We crouched silently in the leaves to wait for my pet chipmunk to emerge from his underground home. We collected oval stones and painted faces on them and called them "Mommy," and "Daddy," and "Nathan," and "Ben," and told stories.

Too soon, it was time for them to leave. Everett, to give Martha and me time for a last chat, took Phyllis out to the yard to help with the raking. Martha and I sat as long as we could, making plans for a reunion at Christmas; it took some of the sting away from parting.

Then they were gone.

"Phyllis had a good time, didn't she?" I asked Everett, as we lolled in the lawn chairs, suffering from postvisit depression.

"The best," he replied encouragingly.

"I wonder what she liked the most? Do you think it was the pony ride?"

"I wouldn't be surprised. Although she sure did enjoy helping you in the kitchen."

I didn't have to wonder long. There was a brief tug-of-war over the first letter to arrive from Martha. "OK," I surrendered. "But read it out loud."

He glanced at the first lines, gave me a strange look, and then began to read, "Dear Folks. Thanks so much for the wonderful week. Phyllis really enjoyed herself. She hasn't stopped talking about—"

Everett hesitated, tried unsuccessfully to suppress a grin, and began again, " 'Thanks so much for the wonderful week. Phyllis really enjoyed herself. She hasn't stopped talking about what fun she had helping Grandpa rake the leaves.' "

7

Roger

"IF YOU ARE RIDING on a Chicago bus after 3:00 P.M. on a weekday," an education professor once informed our class, "you can easily distinguish the teachers from the civilians. The teachers are the ones with the clenched jaws."

I recalled his remark as I stood on the Addison Street subway platform, sandwiched between the roaring traffic lanes of the Kennedy Expressway, at 3:30 on a Friday afternoon; a time when normally I would be home, stretched out on my La-Z-Boy with a bottle of cold soda pop at hand; but today some urgent errand was taking me to the Loop.

"Clenched jaws," the experienced instructor had said. I took my compact out of my purse and peeked. The description was accurate, if skimpy. He should have added "a drained and desperate expression around the eyes." My mirror reflected the look of a lost soul contemplating the third rail.

"Now pull yourself together," I told myself. "Throw back your shoulders, take a deep breath, and uncurl your toes. Remember, you don't have to re-enter the Coliseum until Monday. What's more, you don't have to talk to, smile at, or socialize with anyone under twenty-one all weekend."

The latter reminder did the trick. It dislodged the boulder from between my shoulder blades; it relaxed my eyeballs; it cleaded my sinuses. It did everything but relieve my aching

49

"What did Roger do today, Mom?"

arches; those would have to wait until I snared a seat on the ride downtown.

Above my head, at the street level, a bus disgorged its passengers, and in a few seconds the more athletic came pelting down the stairs to catch the train that was just pulling into the station. Out of the corner of my eye I spied a vaguely familiar hulking figure topped by a friendly, open face and a mop of unruly black hair. I turned to take a second look and was instantly transported six years back in time to a seventh grade classroom where a certain Roger D———— had harassed ten years from my life expectancy. This was Roger, no doubt about it, and instinctively, I looked for a way of escape. It was too late. Not only was I being swept forward by the boarding mob, but I had been discovered. Over the cataract roar of traffic and the throbbing of the train's motor, I heard the booming, slightly incredulous and more than a little triumphant, "Hey, Mrs. Reichel!" I turned a deaf ear and headed for the last remaining seat, hoping that some fellow traveler would fill the gap next to me before Roger could get there; but a couple of pivots, a stiff-arm, a crouching lunge, and he fell into the seat beside me.

"Boy, am I glad to see you!" he thundered.

I smiled weakly, since there was no rejoinder, both honest and polite, that I could offer. The feeling was not mutual. I remembered that the less I had seen of Roger, the happier I had been. His nearness now triggered a painful flashback: frantic notes scribbled almost daily to the third grade teacher across the hall. "Please, Betty, would you take Roger off my hands for a while so I can do some teaching!" Betty never turned me down; she had a Roger whose name was Greg, and I gave her equal time.

"There's something I gotta tell you!" Roger shouted as the train rumbled past the Belmont Avenue station.

Oh, Roger, there always was; and no matter where you were, or what I was doing, you never were able to restrain yourself. In the midst of the pin-drop silence of a math test, you'd shout from your isolated corner of the room, "Hey, Mrs. Reichel! My pencil broke!" I'd point wordlessly to the windowsill sharpener; and you'd clump your noisy, cleated way over there, begin to grind, and then jar the class out of its resumed concentration with, "Hey, Mrs. Reichel! Kin I empty the pencil sharpener? It's running over!"

I'd rise from my desk, mayhem in my eye; and you'd take a feinting step away from the window. Only you wouldn't be finished with me. As soon as all the pencils were moving again; as soon as I relaxed, there'd be that pseudoinnocent, amoral, penetrating voice: "Kin I swat this wasp before it stings somebody?"

There isn't anything you can tell me now, Roger, that I'd be interested in hearing; but since I'm trapped until Lake Street, I'll make a show of civility.

"What is it?"

"Well, I been looking up all my old teachers—"

For what, Roger? To check the rate of survival? I'll wager you sent more than one teacher on a sabbatical leave. It was the year with you that made me switch to high school teaching—a compromise to satisfy my family who wanted me to quit altogether. So you're looking up your old teachers. Why? To deliver the *coup de grace?* Or are you selling vacuum cleaners?

"You see," Roger stumbled on. "I want to apologize."

Of course you do, Roger. Apologizing is your forte. Wasn't it you who spoiled the seventh grade class portrait with crossed eyes, protruding tongue, and horns sprouting from the crown of Mary Jane's head? And didn't you sit abjectly at your desk with tears cascading down your chubby face while I administered a verbal lashing?

And wasn't it you who sent the entire assembly into gales of laughter by dragging a half-beat behind on "Stodola Pumpa," at the same time puffing out your cheeks and pantomiming the motions of a slide-trombonist, safely out of my line of vision as I conducted but in full view of the audience, which that day included the music supervisor? And then later, while being barred from all future programs, didn't you flood the principal's office with evidence of your repentance?

Was there ever a recess—when you were allowed to go out, that is—that you did not return damply contrite, promising to pay for the torn shirt, the uprooted flowers, the broken window? Apologies, Roger, come easily to you. So what's new?

"Something happened to me, Mrs. Reichel."

I straightened up, suddenly interested. Did you finally get your due? Did a no-nonsense shop teacher threaten to run you through a planer? Did the history department gang up on you and put sugar in your gasoline tank? Oh, I could have gone on forever conjuring up punishment to fit Roger's crimes, but he cut into my pleasant reverie.

"I got saved!" Roger blurted out. "I'm a Christian now."

I looked at him, stunned, hardly comprehending. It was a solar plexian blow.

His words began to pour out and tumble over each other now that he had made his most important statement. He spoke about his growing conviction that he was "no good"; how an Awana leader had taken him home after a Friday night meeting—a meeting which Roger had tried to disrupt—and patiently and lovingly explained that God had cared enough for him to send His Son to die for him, to redeem him from that "no-goodness"; that all he had to do was believe in Christ's atoning death and he would be cleansed from his sin and inherit eternal life. He accepted the Lord that night.

This boy who seldom opened a book in my classroom except to vandalize it related how he had been studying the Bible for the last two years "on my own, with the Holy Spirit teaching me."

Roger, thrown out of countless club meetings, described the joy he was experiencing as a leader in that same organization.

Irony of ironies, Roger, who had been returned to school more than once by truant officers, disclosed his plans to go into police work, counseling juveniles!

I sat there gaping, trying to keep up with his enthusiastic testimony. The words, "This is the Lord's doing; it is marvelous in my eyes," kept running through my mind.

Finally I interrupted the eager flow. "Roger, I'm a Christian, too." I wanted him to know that I understood and shared his happiness. It seems he was aware of my convictions, had been ever since I had mentioned during one of our frequent after-school conferences that I prayed for all the children in my class, especially for him.

"That really impressed me," he admitted.

Oh, I had prayed for him. Whether I was inspired by my instinct for self-preservation or by concern for his soul might be argued, but I prayed.

"It was when you sicked Dave onto me that I was really sure you were a Christian," he grinned.

I frowned, puzzled.

"David B——————," he prompted.

It began to come back to me. David had been the most popular boy in the class, in spite of his perfect scholarship. Certain candid observations he had made in his compositions had convinced me he was a Christian and active in his church. Taking him aside one day I suggested to him that Roger needed a friend. Would he take an interest in him? I asked. Invite him to his home? To his AYA activities? Help him with his homework? I let it go at that. I was too bogged down with end-of-the-year duties to follow it up. This testimony of Roger's was the first indication that David had done his missionary work.

I wanted to hear more, but we were nearing my station. I gave Roger my phone number and urged him to call me soon.

When I arrived home that night, I sat down and wrote to my children. "Remember Roger?" I began. That was foolish, they were not likely to have forgotten him; they had had him for dinner five nights a week for an entire school year! "Well," I continued, "he's—" What should I say, I wondered. Redeemed? Transformed? Saved? Born again? "He's a new creature in Christ," I wrote. "Old things are passed away; behold, all things are become new."

Roger did call me and has come to visit us several times, always rejoicing in the Lord, never forgetting to apologize for "the monster I was in your class." On his latest visit he brought a trophy, a brand new convert, another boy from that same seventh grade class.

How grateful I am for that "coincidental" meeting on the subway! The problems I face now in high school teaching are far more complex and difficult to handle than any that Roger presented. I fight a daily battle against discouragement and depression. The Lord knew I needed a booster shot for my ebbing morale. He gave me incontrovertible evidence in Roger's transformation that He listens and "attendeth when I pray."

8
The Years Draw Nigh

EVERETT AND I don't like to admit to ourselves or to the world at large that we are running down. When our children and grandchildren spent their vacations with us in Wisconsin, we tended to set a pretty fast pace, trying to prove our eternal youthfulness and indestructibility. We shocked our offspring out of their sacks at sunrise with Sousa marches on the stereo; we bullied them into joining us for a swim in sixty-five-degree lake water; we dared them to explore new bicycle routes on hilly back roads; we challenged them to croquet tournaments after dinner; and then, at day's end, after we had gotten our second wind, we'd set up the Scrabble game for the survivors.

We did not sport sweat shirts emblazoned "CAMP AWANA" or wear megaphones around our necks, but I'm sure we came across as obnoxious and irrepressible recreation directors rather than the old folks at home.

Our children came to us from their respective concrete jungles pale and tired; they returned home peeling and spent.

They'll never make it to a ripe old age, we worried behind their backs.

"They have no stamina," I complained, not without a touch of smugness. "Why, anything they can do, we can do better, or earlier, or at least with more enthusiasm."

I'm sure we came across as obnoxious and irrepressible recreation directors.

Well, all that was changed last summer. Somewhere between a 5:00 A.M. bird walk and an afternoon excursion to a deer preserve, I ran out of steam. I recognized the need for a long and quiet nap in a cool, shaded bedroom.

"Find the children," I urged Everett. "Tell them I'm canceling out for the rest of the day."

His jaw dropped, consternation in his eyes.

"What excuse will I give?" he asked. There was an uncomfortable silence as both of us tried to think of some nonsenility-connected disability that he could offer as an explanation for my sudden collapse. But neither of us is skilled at improvisations, or prevarications, for that matter. I decided candor was called for—candor and capitulation.

"Tell them the truth," I sighed. "Tell them the old *grandmére,* she ain't what she used to be!"

9

Silas Marner, We Love You

WE'VE ALWAYS BEEN READERS—the children and I. All of us passionately addicted to the printed page. Security in our nursery was not a fuzzy blanket or a teddy bear, but rather a book in hand, or at least within convenient grasp.

By the time they were ready to enter kindergarten, our youngsters had completed the Dick and Jane circuit; and they were standing on tiptoe to pay their own library fines at the age of six. The highlight, the peak of each week, was the Friday night trek to the Humboldt Park Library via our battered Radio Flyer wagon. Only measles, mumps, or blatant insubordination prevented any of the kids from participating in this excursion. To be left behind was heartbreak.

Oh, it wasn't that we were rearing a quartet of geniuses with built-in, insatiable curiosities. Not at all. Our children were quite average. What was not average were our circumstances. We were poor. "Poorer than average," I remind them now years later. They scoff; they remember only that they were happy.

"We were terribly poor," I insist. "As poor as the *Five Little Peppers*," I emphasize. "As poor as little Charlie Dickens in the blacking factory." They are unimpressed. To our four young adults, those were the "good old days."

The truth of the matter is, we taught our children to read when they were still lisping and barely off the bottle because of our straitened situation; we were prisoners in a third-floor, porchless, yardless apartment. We had no car—through circumstance. We had no TV—through choice. But books! Ah, we knew that books could become ladders and wings and magic carpets and frigates "to take us lands away!" We lived vicariously but richly; and the children, if I can believe their denials, were unaware of any deprivation.

Then one summer a friend loaned us her cottage located in the wilderness of Michigan's Upper Peninsula. Since Dad had to work and could not go with us, I was more than a little apprehensive about the venture. I am city-born and city-bred, with no Girl Scout training in my background. I knew that if I rubbed two sticks together, I would get nothing but slivers. Creatures that creep, crawl, or fly in my immediate vicinity can reduce me to a quivering pulp. However, the three oldest children—experienced campers—promised to protect me; and for their sakes I resolved to table my irrationalities for a few weeks.

The borrowed cottage, we had been told, was two miles from the nearest town and three miles from a beautiful lake, so we took bikes along—five of them. We packed linens, cooking gear, clothing, first-aid supplies, and some grocery staples. It never occurred to me to pack a few books. It occurred to the children; but, by the time they reminded me, the trunks had been packed, locked, and tied.

"Sorry," I apologized. "Anyway, there wasn't enough room."

Four pairs of eyes reproached me.

"Besides," I added, "we won't need books; we'll be too busy to read."

They were unconvinced.

"There'll be a library in town," I promised.

Everett drove us to the station in a rented panel truck, took care of our baggage, reminded us how lucky we were and how unlucky he was, and then, assuming the wistful mien of an abandoned husband and father, waved us off. I didn't feel fortunate at all; I felt scared and full of unreasonable resentment at being sent into exile.

We were met at the station early the next morning by my friend's cousin. He transported us and our belongings to the cottage. It was an enchanting sight from a distance: the rustic log house built against a hill and surrounded by dense woods. A huge barn, in a state of partial collapse, dominated the clearing; and a long way off—too long, I thought, for young children and frightened mothers—was the outdoor toilet.

There were adjustments to make. A primitive cookstove challenged my ingenuity. Our only source of light was a single kerosene lamp. Our water supply was an open well a couple of hundred feet from the house. The path to the privy was an obstacle course mined with sleeping garter snakes and a family of bumble bees that never slept. But the children's enthusiasm was encouraging.

"We must spring from pioneer stock," I wrote to Everett on the afternoon of the first day, proud of the children's resourcefulness and the fact that I had not yet come apart at the seams. "We are going to love every minute here," I assured my husband. "The tranquility of the place is unbelievable!"

Then night fell. There had been nothing in my experiential or vicarious background to prepare me for the "terrors by night"—the scrabblings, flutterings, squeakings, and moanings as the rodent-tenanted house came to life after dark. I was horrified by the discovery that Tom, Debby, and Martha shared their attic bedrooms with a colony of bats. The children thought it was a "neat" experience. I remembered ghoulish tales of blood-sucking vampires.

Joanna and I slept on a sofa bed in the living room. The

original tenants of that particular piece of furniture were resentful; there was ample evidence that they held nightly conventions on our covers trying to decide how to bell these particular cats.

The beagle that a neighbor loaned us for the duration, "to keep the bears at a respectable distance," was no help; he was just as "spooked" as I was. He shuffled and whimpered and howled and refused to act as escort to the outhouse, his intended function. On the third day he deserted us, and I couldn't say I was sorry. A dog that slept all day and carried on all night was of no use to me in my predicament.

If our nights were long, so were our afternoons. Hordes of insects sent us running for cover well before dinner time. "It would help if we had something to read," I decided. "Something to keep our minds off our before-and-after-dark visitors." Tom and Martha were given the assignment: bicycle into town, find the library, and ransack its shelves. While they were gone, Joanna plumped up the pillows, Deb started a batch of fudge, and I trimmed the wick and replenished the fuel in our one lamp. The anticipation was delicious!

Much too soon, however, we heard the rattle of returning bikes on the gravel road. Dust-covered and flushed with exertion, our two oldest stood before us—empty-handed.

"There is no library," Martha panted. We were stunned by the blasphemy. I remember looking around, surprised to see the snakes still basking, to hear the bees still buzzing in commerce. Surely, the world should have come to an end.

"There is no library," Tom echoed. "Only a post office, a depot, a Red Owl, and three taverns."

This is what comes of being a city girl, I thought—unbelievable naivete! I had assumed that no town is without a library, a grocery store, and a soda fountain.

We had no choice but to carry on as usual, spending our days

Tom came running toward the house, with a book in his hands!

at the beach, our fun in the sun overshadowed by the knowledge that at four o'clock every afternoon, mobilizing insects would drive us indoors where we hid the key and twenty-questioned and charaded until exhaustion took over.

Then on the morning of the fifth day there was a shout from the barn. Tom came running toward the house, excitedly waving a small black object. It was a book! He was tackled and pummeled, tickled and spread-eagled by his three sisters until he relinquished his find—a mildewed but intact copy of *Silas Marner*.

"Is it a good book?" they questioned me. I was rescued by Tom's defiant "It's a book, isn't it?"

We began an in-depth study of the weaver of Raveloe. Chapters were rationed, one a day, and woe unto the greedy culprit who read ahead! At bedtime we gathered around for devotions, followed by an expository session on *Silas Marner*; that is, I read the day's chapter aloud for the benefit of six-year-old Jo.

We dispelled much of the boredom and ignored most of the terrifying "night music" as we dwelt among the "nutty hedgerows of Raveloe", absorbing Eliot's message of the transforming power of love. The night that we closed the book on Eppie's words to Silas, "I think nobody could be happier than we are," we were smitten with homesickness. We decided to start packing that night and return home the next day.

"Are we taking *Silas Marner* with us?" Jo asked.

"In more ways than you suspect," I answered, tucking the slim little volume in among the driftwood and agates.

Silas Marner now sits in obscurity on a crowded bookshelf in our living room, supported on one side by *Adam Bede* and on the other by *Mill on the Floss*. Whenever I feel the need for a bit of nostalgia—and that happens with more and more frequency of late—I reach for that particular volume and riffle the pages. Oh, I know it has to be imagination, but even after fifteen years the potpourri of mildew and mouse seems to waft upward and transport me back in time to that halcyon summer. I hear the rattling of our bikes on the gravel hills as we caravaned to the beach and back each day; the metallic reverberation of thunder during the night, so frighteningly unlike the sound of city thunder; the plaintive "Old Sam Peabody, Peabody, Peabody" of the white-throated sparrow, which Tom insisted was singing "Go, Lane, go, Lane, go"—his school song.

I can see ten-year-old Debby, addicted to Holloway suckers—those awful all-day caramel concoctions—pedalling madly home along the country lanes trying to outdistance the bees who shared her taste and wanted to share her confection. I remember how we would crowd together each night after dark at the little window in the loft after Jo discovered that from there we could see, for a few brief seconds, the lights of the Chicago-bound train as it skirted the far edge of Fish Lake. Oh, homesickness! And I shall never forget the sight of the three sisters, Anna, Alice, and Emma, walking out of the woods on a Sunday morning to drop in on us, for they had heard from their Chicago friends that we might be lonesome. What beautiful Christian hospitality these Finnish women offered us! They are still our friends.

My little copy of *Silas Marner* has strange powers—in my hands, anyway. It resurrects for me those dear dead days beyond recall, and as long as it can do that it will have its special place on my shelf as well as in my heart.

10

Thoughts on Moving Day

I DETEST MOVING. For weeks, even after the new curtains have been hung, and the dishes are arranged on the freshly-lined shelves, and all our mail has finally caught up with us, I still exhibit the restlessness of a cat in a strange attic. It takes a "heap o' living" in a house to make it feel like home to me. But worse than the ordeal of acclimation is the process of moving itself. With each successive uprooting it has become more burdensome, more expensive, the movers more independent, and I have become more vulnerable.

Our first relocation, post-honeymoon, was accomplished on a Saturday afternoon, on foot, with the help of a family friend. Contrast that with our latest move which required several weeks of packing, a consultation with a representative of the cartage firm, an enormous van, a team of piano-moving specialists, three husky weightlifters, and a crew boss. The accretions of thirty years and four children had been formidable; but because seventy-five percent of our worldly goods consisted of books, we hadn't anticipated any serious problems. Strange to say, therein lay the rub.

We had thought that any moving crew would appreciate the fact that our six rooms of furniture consisted mostly of reading material and the shelves on which to stack it. We were mistaken.

We discovered that the moving trade has its prima donnas, sweatshirted and short-tempered, sensitive to the demands of their calling. Our men didn't complain about the oversized refrigerator that had to be inched and grunted along a narrow, twisting staircase to the third floor, nor were they at all distressed by the unwieldy hide-a-bed that began to unfold in their arms on the second story landing. They seemed to take delight, veins bulging, sweat popping, in wrestling the huge, old-fashioned kitchen range up the three flights and through the narrow doorways.

What did bug them were the more than forty boxes of books that had to be carried down from the flat we were leaving, loaded onto the van, unloaded, and then carted up to the new apartment. Running up and down stairs with Raggedy Ann and Seagram cartons, roped by Everett for easy handling and labeled by me for efficient unpacking, apparently embarrassed the movers. That kind of toting required no finesse, no expertise, and very little strain. They were disgruntled because it challenged their dignity and not their masculature.

With the portaging of the first few boxes, the men merely grumbled; then they sought relief in humor. They joked as they met on the stairs about how well educated they would be by the time they had completed this particular job.

"Hey, Mike," Steve yelled over the porch railing. "I just got done with a whole box of Greek!" He was refering to my husband's old textbooks.

"Izzatso?" Mike bellowed. "Me—I'm doin' a little research." He hefted a carton of encyclopedias onto his shoulder.

Steve spotted Dominic starting up the stairs. "Hey, Dom! What you got there?"

"You guys should be so lucky! Two boxes of 'Romantic Lit.'"

It was Dominic who later boasted at the top of his lungs that he expected to have twenty years knocked off his purgatory sentence since he was transporting a box of Bibles and concordances.

It was a warm spring day, windows were open, and I'm sure the neighbors on all sides knew before the morning was over not only the condition of our furniture but also the contents of our entire library, thanks to the running commentary of the men.

When Steve, the vociferous livewire of the crew, had set the last carton of books down on the living room floor, he decided to "take five." Mopping his face, he let his eyes travel over the cases of books that were stacked in the center of the room; then he gave me a quizzical grin and asked, "Seriously, lady, you people read all these books already?" When I answered in the affirmative, he shook his head incredulously. "Then how come you keep 'em?" he wondered. "I mean, like when I get done with a can of beer, I throw the can away."

I laughed. I had a sudden vision of America's highways littered with 'emptied' books; of recycling centers for paperbacks; of fliptop book covers.

I could see that Steve didn't really expect an answer. He had concocted the metaphor merely to poke a little gentle fun. Having gotten his laugh, he returned to work.

That night, lying awake uncomfortable in the strange house, I remembered Steve's question, "How come you keep 'em?" He had touched a sensitive nerve with his implied criticism. I had spent the first fifty years of my life collecting books, and I knew it was high time I began to reverse the process, especially if I wanted my children to mourn my passing fondly and in leisure and not be troubled by weeks of cataloging, inventory, and phone calls to the Salvation Army's pickup department.

My passion for books has caused Everett to refer to me more than once as "my wife, the bookkeeper." He is right. I operate on Ruskin's principle that "if a book is worth reading, it is worth buying. Nor is it serviceable, until it has been read, and reread, and loved, and loved again; and marked, so that you can refer to the passages you want in it."

My childhood copies of such books as *Black Beauty, Heidi, Jane Eyre, Little Women, Alice in Wonderland* fit Ruskin's description; they are dog-eared and spotted with peanut butter and jelly prints. They were on the shelves for years for my children's enjoyment, and now they are stored in the cellar waiting for the grandchildren to catch up with them.

Each spring Everett goes on a dig, foraging among the artifacts and crates in the basement attempting to eliminate and rearrange in order to establish a small work area for himself. Invariably he returns in a pet, frustrated and grimy, demanding equal space and warning that if he doesn't get it there will be a book burning that will light the sky for miles around.

"I declare," he pants at the top of the stairs, "you've got to do something. Those boxes of books are proliferating!"

"All right," I agree. "Let's start by getting rid of your *Greek Lexicon*, the *Matthew Henry Commentaries*, *Strong's Concordance*, and a few other textbooks left over from your student days—"

"Throw out *my* books?" he roars. "Over my dead body!" That challenge, emanating from a sexagenarian, is unfair and calculated to play on my sympathy; but it's effective and Everett knows it. He wins a compromise. We'll table the issue until next spring. "Soon," I assure him, "we can send the *Bobbsey Twins* to Phyllis and the *Sugar Creek Gang* to Ben and Nathan."

He's mollified but not deceived, knowing that by that time another fifty or sixty volumes will have been added to our bookshelves, necessitating the sending of a like number to the underground repository. My husband is familiar with my propensities;

Get rid of my books? Over my dead body!

he learned early in our marriage that my idea of an exciting night on the town is a visit to a secondhand bookstore where I might pick up an eighty-year old edition of *Pride and Prejudice* for 50¢ or an authentic Horatio Alger for a quarter.

I have a handy defense for my obsession—I teach high school English; but my defense is an ostensible one, high school being what it is nowadays and students being what they are. My real reason for surrounding myself with the books I love, for not discarding them after one reading, for haunting book sales for coveted volumes, is that I find them a source of continual joy. I return to old books as to old friends—to recapture a mood, to quicken memories, to make new discoveries.

"How come you keep 'em?" the mover had asked. His question was contributing to my wakefulness. I decided to get up before I disturbed Everett with my tossing and turning. I groped my way through the unfamiliar darkness to the living room where the street lights shone in through the uncurtained windows.

I curled up in an arm chair and tried to pick up my thinking where I had left off. Poquito appeared from nowhere and jumped into my lap. "That makes two of us who are homesick, baby," I whispered. I comforted her for a moment with a little dog-talk and ear-scratching, and then the question returned and the soliloquy resumed.

How come I keep them? C. S. Lewis said, "An unliterary man may be defined as one who reads books once only." Well, I shall need his and Ruskin's support if it ever comes to a showdown, I thought as I contemplated the stacks of boxes. Those two would appreciate my love affair with books. They would know what I mean when I say a book comes to life when I open the pages and read; just as a phonograph record is animated by the needle. They would understand me, all right, but would they sympathize with my moving and storage problems? Oh, Everett had a point there when he spoke of microfilming; only who can curl up with a good projector?

Far better to have a photographic memory, I would think. I recalled a futuristic novel that I had read a few months before. It concerned an authoritarian regime in which the leaders ordered the burning of all books, maintaining that reading only confused people and made them unhappy and rebellious. However, in remote areas of that fictional country there were individuals who spent every waking moment memorizing entire volumes before the books could be destroyed. These refugees from a godless society had mastered the art of perfect concentration, shutting out all distraction, in order to memorize the philosophies that they thought would be the means of salvation for future generations.

That's not unlike what God expects of me, I reflect. He wants me to hide His word in my heart, so that I can be a living epistle for all men to read. Oh, it's a good thing to study the classics, to commit to memory such passages as "Love is not love which alters when it alteration finds" from Shakespeare's Sonnet 116; or to learn "The world is too much with us . . . Getting and spending we lay waste our powers" from Wordsworth's "The World Is Too Much with Us"; or to recite "He who, from zone to zone, Guides through the boundless sky thy certain flight . . . Will lead my steps aright" from Bryant's "To a Waterfowl"; for these are reiterations of God's truth; but it is God's truth itself that must have the preeminence in my life. I must not lose my equilibrium.

Somewhere a dog howls, and Poquito's ears stand erect as she cocks her head at me for permission to respond. Not receiving it, she drops her head down upon her paws and resumes her napping. A good idea. Suddenly, I am tired enough to sleep. And

I am impatient for tomorrow and the unpacking of my books—the surrounding myself with old friends. Shuffling back to the bedroom I bump awkwardly and solidly against a doorframe. Everett is awake, propped up on an elbow.

"I detest moving!" I grumble.

"You'll feel better in the morning," he promises.

11

Never Too Old

I TOOK MY FIRST DRIVING TEST when I was forty-five, and I failed. Through no fault of my own, I might add. Everett and the examiner were to blame; Everett for rushing me, and the examiner for rattling me.

I told Everett I wasn't ready.

"Nonsense," he contradicted. "You've had the best of teachers." He was referring to himself. "And you've driven hundreds of miles without an accident." He was referring to endless, vacant stretches of freeway west of the Mississippi. "And besides, your learning permit expires tomorrow."

"Do you really think I can pass?"

"I know you can."

"My parallel parking leaves much to be desired," I warned.

"Only when you park on the right side of the street. You're OK on the left."

"And I still can't back up in a straight line," I reminded him.

"Yes," he agreed. "I can't undestand that. It's such a simple maneuver, too."

That "simple maneuver" had almost broken up our twenty-six-year-old marriage.

"Left! Left!" he would shout as I started to back down the empty alley behind our house.

"I am turning left!" I would scream.

"Not the steering wheel! The wheels!"

"Which wheels? The front or the back?"

"It's the front wheels that turn, sweetheart," he would remind me through clenched teeth.

"If you would just leave me alone and let me do it by instinct," I would plead. "It's when I think left and right that I get all confused."

"By the time your instinct takes over, you will have run over a halfdozen trash cans or flattened someone's garage."

It was at about this point in every lesson that I would throw in the towel.

"You hate me, don't you?" I would whimper.

"Don't be silly! I love you," he would bellow.

"Then why are you yelling at me?"

"I'm not yelling at you!" he would roar. "I'm just telling you what to do; and if you would do just what I tell you, there'd be no problem!"

"It's no use," I would moan at the end of these sessions. "I'm just too old to learn."

"I'm not yelling at you," he roared.

"You'll do better next time," Everett would promise. But more practice was not the answer. My reversing deteriorated as rapidly as did our teacher-pupil relationship.

"This is ridiculous. I am not ready to take a test," I told Everett as we reported that morning to the Elston Avenue testing lanes.

"Think positively, and keep the wheel steady," he said, pushing me through the door.

It was early in the day, but even so there was a crowd of applicants and their sponsors already on hand. Everett pried my fingers loose from his arm and directed me toward a line where I was given a number and told to wait my turn. I found myself surrounded by teenagers. I envied them their youth, their quick reflexes, their sharp eyesight, their insouciance. Envied? Let's be honest. I resented them with a passion.

The freckle-faced youngster next to me confided that she expected to fail her first time around. It was routine procedure, she informed me, to give sixteen-year-olds a hard time.

"Then what will you do?" I asked.

"Oh, I'll come back tomorrow. They'll pass me then."

I thought it over. If she expected to be failed because of her youth, then couldn't I expect to be slipped through without a hitch because of my maturity? I took heart.

The line, long though it was, moved rapidly, and soon it was my turn. I was turned over to an irascible fellow who grudgingly introduced himself. He did not look the type, I decided, to make allowances for crow's feet and hard knocks. His name was unmistakably Hibernian in origin, and he pronounced it with a heavy brogue. In a moment of weak-kneed disloyalty, I fervently wished the Bible on our dashboard would either self-destruct or turn into a plaster of Paris St. Christopher.

"So you're a school teacher," he said, consulting my application. Something about his intonation told me that he had spent a disproportionate amount of his student days in the discipline office.

I pleaded guilty, adding with a smile, "Only until something better comes along."

Ignoring my pathetic attempt at humor, he ordered: "Repeat after me. 'I am in the left lane—lane number one. At no time must I leave this lane.'"

He had to be kidding, I thought, but I couldn't risk it. I repeated the promise, resisting the temptation to raise my sweaty right hand.

"Start the car!" he snapped.

I did, without a stutter. Betsy was eager to prove herself.

"Accelerate to thirty miles per hour and then put on the brakes."

My goodness, this is going to be easy, I thought. *Whatever had I been afraid of?*

I pressed down on the accelerator, reached the speed he had asked for, braked smoothly, and then waited for further instructions.

"Now," he said. "Back up slowly until I tell you to stop."

I did not imagine it; there was something ominous in his eye. *He knows,* I realized, my heart hammering in my throat. *He knew the minute he saw me. Maybe it's my weak profile, or the manner in which I grip the wheel, or perhaps there are vibes to which he's sensitive; but he's got me pegged as a loser, a nonreverser of the first order.*

I tried to suppress the mounting panic. What was it Everett had said? "Think positively and keep the wheel steady."

I shifted into reverse. No problem there. I flung my right arm over the back of the seat and turned as casually as I could to look out the rear window. I knew my stance was correct; I had watched my husband do this a thousand times. I might even have been able to follow through, if I hadn't seen at that instant the cloud of witnesses, Everett among them, standing on the observation deck waiting for me to back down the course.

Unnerved, I stomped down hard on the gas and began what can only be described as a slalom in reverse. I lunged; I braked. I began again and overcompensated. I braked a second time, turned the wheel sharply to the left, saw it should have been right, overcompensated again—and wished I were dead! The hoarse "Stop!" of my passenger finally got through to me, and I shifted carefully into park.

There was a short silence. Before he could speak, I said, "Well, I guess that's that!" I opened the door and started to step out.

He grabbed my arm. "You'll finish the course," he said.

I got back in. I recognized a sadist. I resumed driving.

We hadn't gone very far when he said, "Lady, what side of the street are you supposed to drive on?"

I had to think. In fact, at this point I had to stop to think. I pulled over. He repeated his question. All my confidence had drained away.

"The right side?" It sounded like a question. It was a question.

"Then what are you doing on the left?"

I considered. Then I remembered.

"You told me to stay in the left lane," I accused him. "You said I was not to leave the left lane!" I repeated triumphantly. I had him there!

"That was back in the starting stretch," he snarled. "Now we're on a simulated highway."

We drove on. Now that I was beyond redemption, it made no difference that I did a beautiful parallel park that was better than the young boy ahead of me who knocked down the two markers. Nor did either of us care that I skillfully maneuvered the car out of the tight square, or that I parked correctly on the hill.

Everett was waiting for me at the end of the course. I slid over and let him take the wheel.

"Don't you want to drive home?" he asked. He's a bullet biter from way back.

"I'll never drive again," I said. I meant it. I had never known such complete humiliation.

He tried to revive my spirits. "Remember Mr. Jonas?" he asked. Of course I did. Charlie Jonas had been a retired army engineer who had worked on the Gatun Locks in Panama and also had had a hand in the construction of Bonneville Dam in Oregon. Single-handedly he had built a two-story home on the Oregon coast, even installing an elevator for his ailing wife. I knew what my husband was leading up to. Jonas, with all his intelligence and technical expertise, had become a legend around Nehalem because of his erratic driving. He drove on a provisional permit since he could neither parallel park nor back up. He also had a strong tendency to wander across the double yellow, a problem that proved to be his undoing—he died from injuries sustained in a head-on collision. "A natural death," the locals called it.

Everett believed—like Alice's Duchess, that "everything has a moral if only you can find it." He found one in the memory of Mr. Jonas.

"Your not being able to back up is not a sign that you are mentally deficient," Everett stated pedantically. "On the contrary, it might be a mental block peculiar only to the very gifted."

"I'll go along with that," I responded when the tears had dried and my voice had steadied. "So I'm a gifted eccentric, but

I'd much rather be a run-of-the-mill housewife with a driver's license."

For three years Everett tried to woo me back to the wheel, but I remained adamant. Even the inconvenience of trying to cash personal checks without a driver's license did not sway me; and as long as my husband and a few of my friends were willing to chauffeur me around the countryside, why should I place myself in double jeopardy?

I began to notice, however, a subtle change in my attitude; I became an insufferable passenger, wondering, sometimes aloud, how my card-carrying contemporaries had ever passed their tests. One crusty, silver-haired pioneer ignored a local stop sign and shot out onto the highway without a pause. Her excuse: "I was here before that sign was!"

I was occasionally chauffeured by a friend who pulled over to the side of the road—any road—in order to finish a sentence. "I can't talk and drive at the same time," she explained. When I was with her, I never initiated a conversation.

Another acquaintance, who was always willing to drive me to school events, could not drive without talking: about the tailgater behind her, the "turtle" ahead, the "demon" passing on her left, whether or not she could make the green light at the next intersection, the ambling pedestrian in her way, the sticky accelerator, et cetera.

But it was the elderly widow who thought that, because she had carefully braked at the stop sign, she was entitled to pull out onto the highway without looking left or right—and whose assumption demolished our car—that made me reconsider.

"I can do better," I thought. "At least, not any worse." I asked Everett if he would take me on again as a pupil. He accepted the challenge.

I passed my written test with a perfect score, obtained my learner's permit, applied myself with a fanatic, now or never zeal, logged umpteen hours of reverse driving, dragged myself out of a sickbed, and with a fever of 102, took and passed my driving exam without incident. I came close to throwing my arms around the examiner and giving him a grateful kiss.

For weeks I could not come down off cloud nine. I had not realized how intense was my feeling of ostracization from the human race until I earned my passport back—my driver's license. Who cared that it revealed my actual age and my approximate weight? I showed it to all and sundry who would hold still. I had not experienced such headiness since my husband, years before, had presented me with a Marshall Field's charge plate.

When license renewal time rolled around three years later, the Secretary of State sent me a safe driving citation. I was in the midst of hanging it in a prominent spot over the living room mantle when Everett walked in. He took a close look at it and snorted.

"A five-mile round trip to the laundromat once a week is not a true test of one's driving ability!"

I centered the matted and framed certificate and charitably chose to hold my peace.

"Especially," he continued, "since you stop driving at the sign of the first snowflake in November and don't take up the gauntlet again until the ice goes out of the bay in April."

I could stand the proud man's contumely. I knew what was rankling him. During that same three-year period he had received several citations himself—of a vastly different nature. And it is difficult for a teacher to see himself overtaken by his pupil; most difficult when the pupil is also his wife.

It appears as though I may have to brave the elements and dent a fender or two before our old harmonious relationship is restored. I may even have to remove the "new driver" sticker from the bumper. The price of detente is exorbitant. I am willing to pay it, but not just yet.

12

The Doll House

WE CALL OURSELVES "semiretired." Meaning he is; I'm not. It happened three years ago when the Railway Express Agency transferred Everett's name from the payroll to the pension roll and handed him a handsome little box with a brass plate on the cover which read:

> In Appreciation
> from
> REA Express
> Upon the occasion of retirement
> after 32 years of faithful and
> conscientious service.

There was no gold watch inside. I looked.
"It's a beautiful box," I said. "It's mahogany, isn't it?"
"Just so long as it's not pine."
"What'll you use it for?"
Everett examined it carefully, inside and out.
"My dentures."

* * *

A couple of my cronies had warned me that I would have problems when my husband retired. I scoffed. Everett was a most adaptable and flexible person, and as for me, nothing would be lovelier than having a husband to come home to after a hard day's work. I anticipated nothing but a luxurious existence of being chauffeured, cooked for, cleaned up after, coddled, and constantly companioned. Just because it hadn't worked out well for some of my friends, didn't mean it wouldn't for us. And I was right—up to a point.

The chauffeuring, the cleaning, and the coddling I lapped up, being at heart a very lazy individual. It was the "constantly companioned" that was my undoing. Poquito, our Chihuahua, was ecstatic at having her master underfoot for twenty-four hours a day, but I wasn't. After seven hours of confinement each day in a high school classroom, I was accustomed to—and needed—time alone for quiet recovery, a private place in which to lick my wounds. Not getting it, I became a little short of impossible to live with. Everett, understandably, began to hobnob with bewitching Samantha Stevens and intrepid Chief Ironside and Gomer Pyle.

I suggested to my husband that he ought to pursue a hobby, one that would take him out of the house occasionally.

"I think," he said, "you are using the wrong verb. Don't you mean get me out of the house?"

I refused to spar. Instead I handed him a brochure advertising the adult education courses offered at a nearby school. I had encircled the woodshop class because I thought he had talent in that direction. Twenty years before he had nailed some boards together for a bookshelf, and it was still standing.

"It will keep your hands from mischief, and it will give me a couple of nights a week to myself," I encouraged.

He was reluctant; it meant sacrificing his favorite TV programs. I reminded him about summer reruns. It would tie him down, he argued. There were books he wanted to read, things he wanted to do.

"Me, too," I overruled.

I waved him off to his first night of school with my
fingers crossed.

He surrendered finally but conditionally, promising only to give it a try.

That first night I waved him off with my fingers crossed. It would not take much—a crowded parking lot, a snippy clerk, a flat tire—to send him home with a change of heart.

But circumstances cooperated. Everett got himself duly registered, sat through the introductory session, and returned enthusiastic, acting as though the whole idea had originated with him. I could see that this handyman of mine, who until now had lived by saw, hammer, and a pair of screw drivers, was captivated by the plethora of power tools that would be at his disposal; and, although he didn't say so, I knew he had been comforted by the presence of other senior citizens in the class. I was quietly jubilant. I thought it a little too soon to disclose my plans for a massive coffee table, a stately grandfather clock, and my long-suppressed desire for a doll house.

Those grandiose delusions suffered a slight setback when Everett brought home his first project, a pegboard game for which neither of us knew the rules. I admired it dutifully and at the first opportunity donated it to the local Lions Club garage sale.

His second offering was a colonial footstool, just the thing for a two-year-old granddaughter to push around from sink to counter to refrigerator.

A chess table modified into a night stand for the spare bedroom followed. So far, so good. He was improving. His work began to develop a patina of professionalism, and his conversation about woods and glues, lathes and routers rang with expertise. I bided my time. Let his enthusiasm and his confidence gain momentum, I decided, before I make my move.

I encouraged him to go ahead and design and execute a distinctive, varigrained fruit bowl. Next I OKed the expenditure of half a month's Social Security check for the forty feet of birch needed for a bookcase. The night that he finished fastening the last brass pull on a handsome bedside chest, I felt the time was ripe. I asked for my doll house. I didn't have to twist his arm. It seemed that his shop teacher had just completed a doll house for his wife. Within eight weeks I had my minimansion, six rooms and an attic, waiting to be painted, papered and furnished. I was enthralled. I had grown up without ever having a doll house—as inconceivable, I thought, as a boy without a bike.

I rushed home from work each day to varnish the floors, to paint the roof, to "plant" the flowerboxes, to hang the wallpaper; and as I decorated, I discovered that I was not alone, that there is an entire world out there dedicated to insuring the happiness of Lilliputian nuts like myself. I found shops and mail order houses that sell wallpaper, plain and flocked; carpets, oriental and rag; framed oil paintings; layer cakes and boxes of carmel corn; mice, and the traps to catch them; grand pianos that play and piano stools that spin; calendars, current and antique; Christmas trees and Easter bunnies; and, of course, dolls, three generations of them—all of these scaled down to $\frac{1}{12}$ life size.

I was awed and tantalized by the amazing market in miniatures, but I could not in good conscience pay such huge prices for such petite merchandise. I would ask Everett to make most of the furniture and accessories, but I had doubts about his ability to work on pieces so tiny and detailed.

He was willing to try. The time seemed opportune. I was just beginning a year's sabbatical leave from teaching, and we were settling into our mobile home in Wisconsin. The summer before, Everett had erected a minibarn on the property, having no inkling then that it would become a factory, fittingly enough for minifurniture.

Every day my husband would disappear into the barn right

after breakfast, emerging dusty and perspiring for lunch and dinner. I left him alone, but a neighbor across the road, his curiosity aroused by the piercing clamor of the circular saw, the lathe, the drill and sander, dropped in to see what was happening. From the fearsome din and the violent vibrations that threatened to lift the barn off its foundation he expected to find something monumental under construction—not the miniscule drop leaf table and matching kitchen chair that Everett held out for inspection on his outstretched palm. He was reminded, the neighbor told my husband, of Aesop's pregnant mountain that labored and brought forth a mouse!

Somewhere along the way "my" doll house became "Phyllis's" doll house. We realized we were getting ready to relinquish it to our granddaughter. We decided that once the last drape was hung, the pots and pans were neatly stacked in the kitchen cabinet, and the tiny flowers were stenciled on the cradle and wardrobe in the nursery, it would need a younger caretaker than ourselves; someone with tiny hands that could wield a four-inch dust mop, and squarecorner the sheets on a wee brass bedstead, and rock to sleep a palmsized baby in the diminutive cradle.

Phyllis was, and still is, impatient to move in. She asked her mother, "How come Grandma and Grandpa are keeping my doll house?"

"It's not ready yet," Martha told her. "Grandma and Grandpa still have a lot of things to do to get it ready for you."

What Martha didn't tell her, since it would have been a little difficult for her to grasp, is that at not quite four she was not quite ready for the doll house. But she believes, because she knows that we would not have told her so if we did not mean for her to have that magic, little house for her very own; and so her audacious assumption enables her to say "my doll house" while it is still a thousand miles away with Grandma and Grandpa.

My granddaughter's impatience reminds me, reprovingly, of a spiritual parallel: I am not nearly so anxious to possess the mansion that is being prepared for me.

"I wish," I confide to Everett, "that I had that same sanctified audacity, that child-faith, to believe Jesus' promise: 'I go to prepare a place for you.'"

"But you do believe it," he chides.

"Not the way I should," I confess. "Not to the point of unbearable suspense."

* * *

We don't bother to apologize for the fact that our own home is neglected while we work on Phyllis's doll house. "First things first," defends Everett. And neither do we make excuses for pursuing such a simple hobby. We've encountered too many envious friends. In fact, one of those friends, a person I had considered a confirmed spinster, says she is now on the lookout for a middle-aged, unmarried cabinet maker, preferably a man with a bit of whimsy in his makeup, so that he's not above carpentering a doll house. I suggested to her that she enroll in a woodshop class. Then, one way or the other, she'll get her petite *maison*.

13
A Glorious Way to Go

I REFUSED TO GO IN. My husband and I had been sitting outside a Chicago ski shop for an uncomfortable half hour while I dug in my heels and lifted my voice in protest. The whole thing had been my idea in the first place, he reminded me, and now I was balking.

"You know how you are," he argued. "We have to push you into the pool every summer and then threaten to pull the plug to get you out."

"This is different. Who ever heard of a fifty-year-old grandmother, and a three-time loser at Weight Watchers, taking up skiing?"

"It's only cross-country skiing," Everett reasoned. "You're not going to tackle the Swiss Alps!"

"I'm not in condition to tackle a waxed linoleum, and neither are you. You and I are old folks who should be at home. We're dentured, bifocaled, stiffjointed, dull of hearing. First time out, one of us will die in a tangle of splintered birch, impaled on our poles."

"It would be a glorious way to go," he grinned. "How many children can boast of a grandparent who perished in a ski mishap?"

I forced a tepid smile. "You really want to go through with this, don't you?"

He did. He pointed out that he was tired of losing to me at Scrabble; that bird-watching had begun to pall; and moreover, winter weekends were looming.

I capitulated. I left the warm security of our station wagon and with a little assist from Everett entered an emporium of instant intimidation. The ski shop reeked of youth and recklessness. It was unrelieved outdoorsman. It was no place for a bunioned, sinusitic hausfrau like myself.

The salesman, a lithe Jean-Claude in a turtleneck, did a doubletake at our entrance and then busied himself elsewhere. For this I was grateful. In Marshall Field's I could have pretended that I was taking a shortcut from housewares to gardening supplies by way of the sporting goods section, but in this watered-down Abercrombe and Fitch no one would believe that I was lost between escalator stops.

I tugged at Everett's sleeve. "If anyone asks, we're shopping for a gift for one of the children."

He didn't hear me. He was racing toward a rack of brightly varnished skis. It was apparent from his expression that he was entertaining visions of gemuetlichkeit and fondues, aprés ski togs and roaring fireplaces—all the romantic fantasies engendered by TV commercials.

Lifting a ski from the rack, he stroked it affectionately, turned it tenderly in his hands, ran a finger lightly along its bowed edges, and murmured ecstatically, "Look at the beautiful camber. These are the ones I want."

The only camber he knows anything about, I reflected disloyally, is found at the base of his Salem rocker.

The salesman returned; apparently his curiosity had won out. My husband shifted the ski he had been fondling and said with a *savoir faire* that was meant to impress—and a stilted construction that immediately destroyed the impression—"We would like to be outfitted with some cross-country ski equipment."

"Well, then," the young man said, wresting the ski from my husband's grip, "in that case, you'd better come this way. You're looking at a downhill ski; the cross-country gear is on the other side of the shop."

Our innocence had been discovered. From this point on we were to be clay in the clerk's hands, and all three of us knew it. He dispensed with a sales pitch. He didn't defer to our taste or our intelligence. Rather, he prescribed: "You'll need this, that, these, and those."

Within a half hour he had finished with us; and there it all was, spread out on the counter and propped against the register, the incriminating evidence that nothing can compare with an old fool's foolishness. Our impedimenta consisted of skis and bindings, boots, mittens, and one tin of wax.

"How long will this wax last?" Everett inquired.

"Oh, it will take you through the winter."

We trusted his judgment. At the time we knew no better. In retrospect we can only assume that he was convinced the wax would outlast our enthusiasm.

We began our adventure in a lonely picnic grove in Door County's Peninsula State Park, an area sufficiently isolated that I could lose my dignity and yet maintain my public image. That we were far removed from phone and fracture ward seemed of secondary importance.

We donned our skis. My husband, once. I, twice. No one had told me that there were a right and a left ski! I leaned heavily on my poles and watched Everett strike out on his own. My heart sank. He was a natural! Swooping and gliding, he rode his skis like a pro, albeit slightly pigeon-toed.

"Tremendous!" I shouted in a display of good sportsmanship and immediately found myself spread-eagled in the snow, sans skis and sans poles. I floundered to my knees and after several spine-wrenching attempts managed to get myself back into my gear and on my feet.

Everett skimmed past. "Are you all right?" he asked, trying hard to appear solicitous.

"I'm fine," I shrugged, trying hard to appear nonchalant. Shrugging was a mistake. This time I landed on my face, with a ski tip embedded in my ribs. Again there was the frustrating, ankle-bending struggle to disentangle and reassemble—not only myself, but a right ski and a left ski, a right pole and a left pole, a right mitten and a left mitten.

"And a right and a left to the jaws of those outdoor evangelists who insist that anyone who can walk can most assuredly ski!" I muttered.

Those first few weeks I was never without a stiff shoulder or wry neck and sported contusions in various stages of absorption. Let it be a matter of record, however, that I persevered. Each weekend I shucked the security of my orthopedic oxfords and became apodal: instead of on feet, I moved about on six-foot-long pedal extremities: "Skids," I labeled them. "Have to grease my skids," I would sigh, reaching for our tin of rapidly diminishing wax.

We measured my progress by the decrease in the number of falls; a no-fall weekend was a cause for celebration: marshmallows in my hot chocolate! Gentle genuflections that occurred on hummocks, and from which I could rise easily, were discounted. An experienced skier, trying to be helpful, suggested, "Tuck in your butt, suck in your gut, and plant your poles behind you." I put the vulgar little formula into practice, insofar as I was able, and found that it worked. Often.

We signed up for a series of lessons in January, ostensibly to encourage the young teacher. Actually, we wanted to enlarge our knowledge. That is, I did. Everett, already proficient, wanted to enlarge his audience.

Our instructor was a red-bearded, hollow-cheeked Mother Earth disciple named Steve. Our classroom was a cluttered combination bike, ski, and natural foods shop in Fish Creek. I inferred from the unwashed wok pans in the kitchen that it was also Steve's pad.

Our first lesson was concerned with the selection and care of skis. I braced myself for boredom. After all, we were veterans. But our guru-of-the-skis was a born teacher and had me spellbound from the start.

Steve sat on the floor, backlighted by the morning sun shining through a transplanted stained glass window, and led us step by step through the rituals of ski care. He demonstrated the laborious stripping of the lacquer from the new ski, then the fine sanding, next the sealing with pine tar using a propane torch, and finally, the waxing. *Mea culpa,* I gulped. We had done none of these things.

Arranging a palette of tins and tubes of waxes, Steve explained how they were color keyed to snow and weather conditions; how the right wax or combination of waxes made it possible to climb almost any kind of slope, to skim rather than plod, to avoid bogging down in wet snow on warm days.

Everett and I exchanged glances. We were both remembering the callous salesman who had sent us out into the world armed with a single tin of wax. Too, we were beginning to realize that it would take hours to get our skis into shape before the next lesson.

I had a sudden inspiration. "Wouldn't it be possible, Steve, for us to bring our skis in and have you recondition them?" I asked.

We hadn't related to our skis at all. We were guilty, in fact, of ski abuse.

"It would," he answered. "But I don't recommend it." He paused, and his voice became gently reproving. "I think it's most important that a skier relate to his skis."

I blushed at my blasphemy and retreated into my corner as seven pairs of eyes, including Everett's, reproached me.

The lesson finished, Steve asked us to get our skis so that he could look them over. I felt suddenly ill. Everett and I hadn't related to our skis at all; in fact, we were guilty of ski abuse. We had scoured them on icy snowmobile trails; we had gouged them traveling over gravel-peppered snow on isolated back roads; we had splintered the edges climbing over tree stumps in dense woods.

I flinched as Everett handed our mutilated skis to Steve. I held my breath while his sensitive fingers moved gently over the pitted surfaces, tracing the cruel abrasions. Steve finished his inspection and then hesitated, searching for the right words. Then he grinned—warmly, admiringly. "Say," he said. "You folks have really been skiing!"

It was absolution and benediction all rolled into one! Tension snapped. Words poured forth. We backed Steve into a corner and related the story behind every scratch and scar. He listened, empathized, sold us a blowtorch and pine tar, scrapers and daubers, an assortment of waxes with a backpack to carry them in, and a copy of *The New Cross-Country Ski Book,* and sent us on our way—to sin no more.

The winter passed too swiftly. For the first time in our lives we were not anticipating spring.

"I think we are hooked," I confided to our children in our weekly newsletter.

"We rather suspected as much," my oldest daughter wrote caustically. "You keep forgetting to ask about the grandchildren until the postscripts."

We realized the totality of our commitment on a Saturday morning in February when we arose, glanced at the thermometer which registered a plus five, listened unconcernedly to the winds howling about the eaves, and then without a backward glance, picked up our skis, and struck out on a prebreakfast tour.

We began to seek converts, even proselytized. A faculty crony, who happened to be an avid downhill skier, queried impatiently, "What do you see in crosscountry skiing?"

I chose to misinterpret her question and answered her literally. "One day we coasted down a forest trail and came face to face with a doe," I said. "We skim along beaches where sand has been crystallized into huge lumps of maple sugar. We pole our way along aisles of abandoned apple orchards where orange-hued, frozen fruit hangs from snow-laden branches—"

But I lost her. She is Physical Ed. I am English Lit. She cannot understand our fascination with the delicate traceries of rodent and bird tracks, hieroglyphics in the snow, or our excitement at hearing the distant thunder of ruffed grouse bursting into flight within arm's reach. And surely she would question my emotional stability if I confided that often, overcome by the grandeur of it all, I stop along the trail, breathless and teary-eyed, and whisper, "God, Your world is too beautiful today!"

Sometime around April the rains washed away the last vestiges of snow, and the ice moved out of the bays in our northeastern Wisconsin refuge, and we had to accept the fact that there was little chance of a late spring blizzard. Cantankerous as a pair of bears just out of hibernation, we took to our bikes to work off our frustration. Oh, how tedious and tasteless in comparison to skiing is cycling!

In May Everett persuaded me to store the skis in a closet, promising I could take them out occasionally to do a little relating. The waxes, a dozen aromatic tins, I placed in my dresser drawer, like a pomander among my lingerie. I comforted myself with the knowledge that, since summer was almost upon us, winter couldn't be far behind.

"And if we become desperate in our doldrums," I joked, "there's a scuba diving school at Gill's Rock—"

Everett sat up, immediately captivated by the idea.

"Don't be silly," I headed him off. "Think of the absurdity of a fifty-one-year-old grandmother taking to the waves in flippers and goggles and a size twenty-and-a-half rubber suit. Why, the first time out, I'd get tangled in the seaweed and drown."

I knew what his retort would be, something about our grandchildren being able to boast about their grandparents dying romantically at sea. The dialogue was strangely familiar. This was where I had come in. The question was Did I want to stay around and see if there would be any changes in the script?

Thirty years of married life have taught me that distraction is the better part of valor. "I'm about to bake a pie. Would you like cherry or apple?" I asked.

14
One Wife's Complaint

EVERETT IS ILL. Nothing serious, just a case of the flu. Not even a serious case, it merited no more than a "hot tea-aspirin-bed rest" prescription via telephone from our overworked physician.

"How is Dad?" a daughter calls to ask.

"How should I know?" I reply, a bit on the peevish side. "He's taken to his bed and barricaded the door from the inside."

"You should be used to that by now," she laughs. "Isn't that his usual pattern?"

It's his usual pattern, all right. The whole family—I'm the only holdout—accepts the fact that when illness strikes, Dad turns his face to the wall and asks for nothing more than to be left alone. He suffers in stoical silence behind closed doors and doesn't emerge until the malady has run its course.

They say I shouldn't complain; that I should be grateful; that I should remember all the women who have a different tale to tell, who are married to overgrown boys who demand intensive care for an ingrown toenail or who insist on round-the-clock nursing for a head cold. Well, for the record, let me say I envy those women. I would love to be able to identify with the compassionate ladies on TV commercials who spoon out cough medicine to their sneezing, raspy-throated husbands and are told, "You're a good wife, honey"; or with those who with healing in their fingers rub ointment into the aching shoulders of their appreciative mates; or with the efficient helpmates who keep a bottle of sleeping tablets handy in the bedside table for the insomniac husbands who have important business dates the next morning. But unfortunately for me, Everett concocts his own cough syrup out of a mixture of honey and lemon, and soaks away his muscular aches and pains in a steaming tub, and has never permitted a worry to rob him of a minute's sleep. There is nothing one can do for a do-it-yourselfer, except as Everett suggests, "take care of yourself, get enough sleep, exercise regularly and take a vitamin every morning, just in case."

"Just in case what?" I ask.

"Just in case I ever do need a nurse."

"Fat chance!" I reflect. Why, I haven't fluffed up his pillows, sponged his fevered brow, or prepared tempting invalid trays since the first year of our marriage when he came down with "la grippe." Looking back, I have to admit that I may have overreacted at the time, but I was motivated by fears of an early widowhood. Throughout the three-day siege I rarely left Everett's side, convinced that if I did, he would quietly slip away. When his temperature "soared" to 101, I begged to be allowed to summon a doctor, preferably a Harley Street specialist.

"Only if I take a turn for the worse," he smiled weakly.

I wrung my hands. "How will I know?"

"Keep an eye on my toes," he whispered. "They'll begin to turn blue."

He was needling me, of course, since I refilled the hot water bottle so frequently and enthusiastically that his nether extremities were a permanent scarlet and threatening to peel.

To keep up his strength I plied him with gelatins and softboiled eggs and graveyard stews. "You have got to eat," I pleaded. "You'll feel better if you do."

He made the effort, but gave up, groaning, "You better. Me worse."

On the third day he staggered to his feet, claiming I left him no alternative: if he stayed in bed any longer, he would make medical history by dying of an overdose of TLC. That was his prognosis. It was my opinion that his rapid recovery was due to my dedicated nursing.

At any rate, he wasn't to receive such devoted care again for a long while. Our family began to grow, and any manifestation of illness that Everett displayed was quickly upstaged by the more dramatic chicken pox, mumps, measles, rheumatic fever, polio, rheumatoid arthritis, and the thousand natural germs that our children were heir to. I have shadowy recollections of Everett seeking medical treatment for a wrenched back, a sprained ankle, sporadic cases of the flu—but only out of the corner of my mind as I tended the children.

Then after twenty-seven years we were alone again, back where we had begun—in a strangely silent house with a medicine cabinet that was almost bare. It was an unhappy time of life for me, that anticlimactic period of despondency, that after-the-ball-is-over depression, when a woman becomes conscious of her supernumerary role. I needed to be needed. I would have welcomed a broken leg or a peptic ulcer if Everett had brought either home from work. I was ready to seize on a sneeze or gloat over a goutish digit to give meaning to my existence. Try as he might, Everett could not accommodate me. It was a period of unprecedented good health, until one day he came home with the news that he needed another hernia repair.

"How many is that?" I asked. "Your third or fourth?" My vagueness was understandable since his previous surgery had been overshadowed by more demanding family emergencies. His third, he informed me; and if he had anything to say about it, it would be his last. And, since it was just a routine job of hemstitching, there was no cause for me to try to make an occasion of it or to become overly solicitous, he warned me.

His cautionary words had the opposite effect; they triggered an alarm. My suspicions mounted when I noticed he was cleaning out his dresser drawers and organizing his papers and prepaying some bills.

It was the fuses, though, that really sent me into a panic. "You ought to learn where the fuses are and how to change them," he said kindly but firmly, taking me down to the basement the day before he entered the hospital. He is getting his house in order, I thought. He is concealing something far more serious than a recurring hernia. But if he could be brave, then so could I. I stiffened my lip and listened to his parting instructions as attentively as I could under the circumstances—the circumstances being that his detailed directions sounded to me like deathbed dicta. There was nothing Everett could have said to me at this point that would have convinced me he was not riddled with malignancies.

I had promised that I would stay away from the hospital until the surgery was over and he was out of the recovery room. I had not, however, promised to abstain from besieging the switchboard with anxious queries. I suppose that's the reason they had the surgeon phone me with reassurances.

"Then it was only his hernia? You didn't find anything else?" I asked fearfully.

There was a long pause.

"What was it you had in mind?" the doctor asked dryly, intimating by his sarcastic tone that, if I would be more specific, he might be inclined to go back and look.

"Nothing," I mumbled, thoroughly ashamed of myself. I hung up and returned to the bag I was packing for Everett with a few odds and ends I intended to take on my first visit: his Indian blanket bathrobe, flannel pajamas, a pair of down-at-the-heel mules, magazines, fresh fruit, and snapshots of the grandchildren. The latter item, the photos, were to remind him and the nurses that he was not as young as he looked.

That first visit lasted an hour. I had come prepared to spend the day: to coax him out from under the covers, to plump his pillows and to moisten his parched lips with a pipette, to complain about the lack of service in general and the shortage of blankets in particular, to crank the bed, to organize the clutter on the bedside table, to shave his jowls if necessary. But when I walked into his room, there was no neglected silent sufferer needing my ministrations. Someone had gotten there before me. My husband, clean-shaven and glowing, was sitting in an armchair, not much the worse for wear. I tried to conceal my disappointment.

"Say, am I glad you came!" he smiled, seizing my hand.

I brightened. He had missed me after all.

"I'm broke," he went on to explain. "I had to have the barber give me a shave, and I have to pay for my share of the TV rental, and the newspaper costs twenty-five cents a day, and they're taking up a collection for the head nurse who's getting married next week."

Ah well. I handed him my wallet and told him to take what he needed. "Just leave me bus fare," I asked. I started to unpack the goodies I had brought when we were interrupted by the entrance of a pretty librarian pushing a book and magazine cart. Everett checked out enough literature to last him through several operations.

No sooner had the bookmobile disappeared through the door when a pert young aid wheeled in a refreshment trolley. Everett helped himself to cheese and crackers and pineapple juice, "for now," he said, and a couple of cartons of chocolate milk "for later." Before I could begin to remonstrate, a kitchen staffer was at his elbow with the next day's bill of fare on which my husband was asked to check not only his preferences but the size of the portions, small or large. From where I sat, I could see that Everett did not intend to stint.

The beauteous and engaged head nurse dropped in next, yawning widely to emphasize her declaration that she was worn out attending one shower after another, and expressing regret that none of the afflicted in this particular ward would be able to attend the ceremony on Saturday. The four old men were charmed by her performance which was interrupted by the arrival of a probationer come to take temperatures. We had barely begun to talk about the operation when a garrulous cleaning woman did a turn around the room with a dustmop. During all this activity I tried to keep a smile on my face and my feet out of the way.

"I guess I'd better start for home," I said making no attempt to disguise my desolation.

"You might just as well," he agreed, insensitive to my misery.

"The buses will be crowded," I reminded him, picking up the pair of shopping bags I had never gotten around to unpacking.

"Yes, they will," he nodded, impatient for my departure.

"Besides, my sinuses are killing me," I tried, knowing that was usually good for a comforting word or two.

"Must be the stuffy air. You'll feel better when you get outdoors," he hinted.

It was not the stale air. It was the head nurse's Shalimar perfume. I started for the door.

"Before you go, would you do something for me?" he asked.

I spun around. Would I? Just name it. Your slightest wish—

"Would you turn on the TV? Channel 2. 'Bewitched' has been on for the last couple of minutes." He couldn't eliminate the reproach in his voice. "Be a shame to miss it; especially since you're leaving anyway."

I rode down in the elevator with another hospital "widow."

"They have a much better system in Africa," I confided, still smarting from my rejection. "The family moves in with the patient."

"Oh, dear me, I wouldn't like that at all," she murmured. "I'm enjoying the rest."

I made another attempt on the crosstown bus. "It's inhumane," I complained to my seatmate. "What it amounts to is that the hospital has taken my husband into custody and I am allowed visiting privileges."

She said placatingly and with a sympathetic smile, "Well, he'll be home soon. Didn't you say it was only a hernia?"

"But he'll be practically well when he gets home—" I began, but her unlifted eyebrows stopped me. Clearly she had me categorized as an odd one.

I phoned my daughter when I reached home. "I don't think I'll go back for another visit. There's no need."

"That's good," she said. "Then there's nothing to worry about."

"That's the trouble," I wailed.

"That's the trouble," I explained to Everett when he had been home a few hours. "I'm being prevented from fulfilling my marriage vow: 'To have and to hold, to love and to cherish, in sickness and in health.' When you get sick you either go to the hospital where you hide behind a half dozen antiseptic attendants or you stay home and lock yourself in quarantine!"

He said he saw my point, and he promised that he would put himself in my hands the very next time he fell ill.

I didn't have long to wait. That was the year of the Hong Kong flu. Everett, trailing his moth-eaten blanket robe, headed

"Do I need all that for a sneeze?"

for the isolation ward. "Oh no you don't," I said, jamming my foot in the door. "I'm in charge, remember?"

I arranged the nostrums and various sickroom utensils on the dresser, a pitcher of lemonade and a box of tissue on the bedside table. I pinned a paper sack to the side of the mattress, lowered the shades, filled the icebag for his head and plugged in the heating pad for his feet. I dashed to the dime store and bought a small handbell that he could ring for service. When I wasn't in his room changing sheets or forcing liquids or taking his temperature, I was cleaning and polishing up a storm in the rest of the house. I was happily fulfilled—for one whole day.

Then on the morning of the second day I sat on the edge of the bed and said, "Move over, honey." I was burning up with fever. Every symptom that Everett had displayed, I had improved upon. We lay there, partners in pain, taking turns at squeezing lemons and filling icebags.

Eventually, my husband recovered. I didn't. I advanced to double pneumonia. That was all the evidence Everett needed to prove his point—that he was justified in keeping me out of the sickroom.

"From now on you will limit your practice to first aid," he ordered.

"Slivers?" I asked hopefully.

"Only those in inaccessible places," he qualified.

"Foreign objects in your eye?" I asked.

"Wednesdays and Sundays only."

I continued to haggle. "Temporary splints?"

He gave it some thought. "If we're miles from human habitation in the dead of winter, yes."

I decided to be content with the compromise and to table the topic of tourniquets until some future discussion.

Months have passed since our agreement; and while I have

been assiduously studying my first aid manual, Everett apparently has been living more cautiously than ever, managing to avoid even such commonplaces as spattered grease burns and thumbtack punctures.

As I write this, he is lying in bed ill. Nothing serious. Just a mild case of the flu. It merits no more than a "hot tea-aspirin-bed rest" prescription via telephone. I decide to go out and have my hair done and do a bit of window shopping.

"Before you go," Everett calls from the bedroom, "come in here a sec." Wordlessly, he hands me the childproof aspirin bottle. I turn the cap till the arrows line up, press my thumb on the red dot, give it a half-twist to the left and pour out his dosage. Gratefully he pops them into his mouth and accepts the glass of water to wash them down.

"You're a good wife, honey," he murmurs, sinking back against the pillows.

"I know," I agree happily. It's so nice to be needed.

15

Of Benches and Pews

IT WAS ONLY NATURAL that my thoughts should turn to benches and pews this morning for there had been a pleasant surprise awaiting us in the little country church where we frequently worship. Handsomely covered foam rubber cushions had been installed since our last visit. For old bones, I muse; like Everett's and mine. And it's about time! Asceticism and austerity and hard pews were all right when I was young, but the ravages of rheumatism and old age have gradually transformed me into a voluptuary. I long ago turned in my haircloth and sandals for pile linings and crepe soles. I have become partial in my declining years to velvet housecoats and soft sweaters, electric blankets, air conditioners, and recliners. *I grab all the comfort I can get,* I reflected, as I settled back for a few minutes of quiet meditaiton before the morning service.

Ours is a mannerly congregation for the most part. The hellos are said and the news is exchanged in the vestibule; the sanctuary is what its name implies. My mind is free to wander undisturbed before the pastor mounts the pulpit and the Doxology calls me back to attention.

My reveries of late tend to be retrospective, one of the syndromes of advancing age that I am reluctant to accept, along with aching joints and graying hair. At any rate, this morning I think of pews and benches, realizing with a shock of recogni-

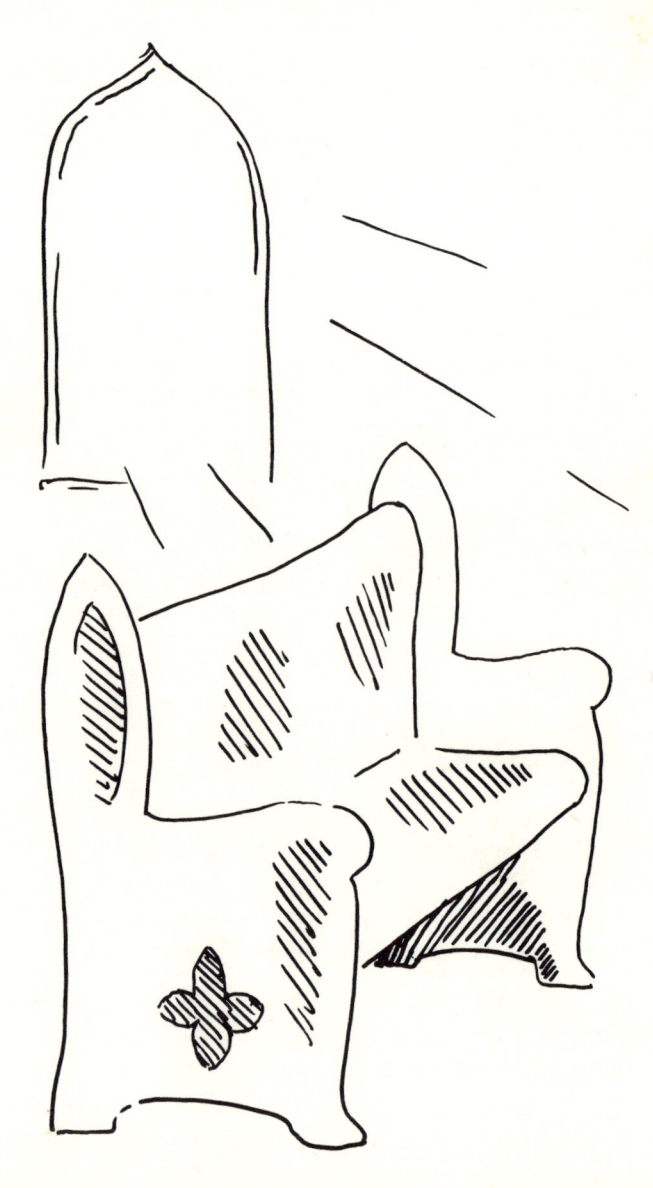

My moments of decision have come to me while sitting still.

tion that the crises of my life could be listed under the heading "Benches I Have Known." My moments of decision, my epiphanies, have come to me while I was sitting still.

No one will ever install a bronze plaque on a certain pew in Judson Baptist Church, a plaque reading: "Jocelyn Sat Here," but that's where it all began thirty-five years ago. "Strait is the gate and narrow is the way which leadeth unto life, and few there be that find it," was the text that morning. It was the minister's custom to give an invitation after each message. I didn't know that. As far as I was concerned, the whole event had been staged for my particular benefit: the setting, the songs, the sermon, and the invitation. I raised my hand, not quite certain what it was I was responding to but assured for the first time in my life that God loved me, that Christ had died for me, and that I was going to be one of those few to enter in at the "strait" gate. Nobody had ever been more ready to raise his hand at an invitation than was I. I didn't see it then (of course, I did later) that the Lord had been laying the groundwork for a long time. Small coincidences, chance acquaintances, and insoluble home problems—He was working these together for my good.

I was born into a nominal Roman Catholic home, lived in a Catholic neighborhood, and enrolled in a Catholic school; so it is not surprising that I was eleven years old before I had any real contact with a Protestant. Pauline was one of three non-Catholics in my sixth grade class, and she invited me over after school one day. I can still recall the cold, frothy milk in blue glasses; graham crackers stacked on matching plates; a lovely, friendly mother; and an air of order and tranquility such as never existed in my own home and which made me ache with envy. When they invited me to a children's evangelistic meeting, I accepted out of curiosity. I was allowed to go only after promising my mother I would not take an active part in the meeting.

During the prayers, I sat stiffly upright, eyes wide open, a superior smile on my face. While the others sang catchy choruses, I kept my lips tightly closed, unaware my swinging legs betrayed me. I recited a rosary to myself while a chalk talk was presented. At the end of the service I congratulated myself, convinced I had come away unscathed. I had not. A tiny chink had been made in my prejudice.

The chink widened and a little more light penetrated a year or so after that. I was stopped near my home one afternoon by a bonneted, grandmotherly woman who thought she recognized me as one of the neighborhood children who relieved their summer boredom by singing taunting verses into the open windows of the Salvation Army chapel during the meetings. I refused to admit my complicity. If she had shown the least bit of malice, I might have boasted of it; but she was kind and soft-spoken and had smiling eyes. I resisted her seductiveness, maintaining stoutly, "I'm a Catholic!" as though that granted me a special dispensation and absolved me from all guilt. I ran from her presence and saw her no more, but let it go on record that I never again joined the neighborhood glee club!

In my junior year I transferred to a public high school. The reason I gave my family and myself was that I had my eyes on the editorship of the public school newspaper which had five times the circulation of the parochial publication. The real reason—the one that I was not at all aware of—was that God, who had begun a good work in me, was continuing to perform it. At the new school there was a student the Lord wanted me to meet.

Minette had the same inner peace, the same aura of tranquility that had filled me with such longing in Pauline's presence six years before. We became good friends. I respected her stand, but her low-keyed attempts to witness or to get me out to church were unsuccessful. I did not think the answer to my problems—and they were many and serious at the time—lay in a change of church address.

Then, shortly after high school graduation, while I was a probationer in nurse's training a hundred miles from Chicago, I began reading the Bible with a senior nurse, a Christian girl from Tennessee. I felt the first stirrings, the spiritual labor pains. I phoned Minette. "I am coming home this weekend," I said. "May I go to church with you Sunday morning?"

So there I sat, and the minister was faithful, and I raised my hand at the invitation, and everything began to fall into place. Spiritually, that is. Materially, my world fell apart.

"If you could have seen," someone asked me, "the inquisition that lay ahead, the harassment, the expulsion from school (justified because I was in a Roman Catholic institution on a scholarship), would you have made the same decision?"

"If I could have seen all that," I replied, "then I would also have been able to see the salvation of my mother, brother, and sister. I would have thumbed my nose at the sufferings of that present day," I laughed.

And besides, if it had not been for my experience in that church pew in the Chicago suburb, then there would never have been the bench in Humboldt Park two years later.

Everett and I were newly engaged. He had dropped in unexpectedly one afternoon carrying a paper sack containing a pint of strawberry ice cream.

"Get a couple of spoons," he ordered, "and hurry!"

I ran a comb through my hair, picked up the silverware, and followed him at a breakneck pace down the stairs and onto a streetcar. In five minutes we were at the park, catching our breath on our favorite bench.

"A pint of ice cream for the two of us?" I gasped as he opened the bag.

"I didn't have enough money for a quart," he apologized.

"We make a pint do for the whole family," I went on to explain.

"Stop talking and eat," he urged. "It's melting fast."

I applied myself diligently for a while.

"How come this impromptu picnic? You're supposed to be studying for a test," I reminded him.

"We have something important to talk about."

"What?"

"Us." He assumed a stern expression that was not quite successful considering the dollop of ice cream on the tip of his nose. I started to reach for my hanky, then a premonition made me pause. Why was he so grave? Had he changed his mind about us? It would be understandable if he had, I admitted to myself. He was a Moody student, surrounded by the feminine cream of God's crop—girls who knew chapter and verse, proper skirt lengths and cosmetic taboos—and I was a relatively new convert, unschooled and gauche in my Christian walk. "No, I can hardly blame him for reconsidering," I conceded grudgingly, deciding to let him go through the rest of the day with a frosted nose.

I braved the question. "What about us?"

"Our love," he said. "We haven't surrendered it to the Lord." My heart plummeted. It was true, I concluded. He had second thoughts. He wanted out. He was going to use a pious excuse to jilt me. I fought back the mounting panic and decided to argue my case.

"I prayed. For weeks after I met you, I prayed that, if God didn't intend us for each other, He would keep you from becoming interested in me." I didn't think it necessary to add that, while I was praying so selflessly, I kept sticking out my foot for Everett to trip over.

He considered, shifting the sodden ice cream carton in his hands.

"That's not quite the same thing. This is something we have to do together. We have to make sure this is what God wants for us; and if it isn't, we have to be willing to give it up."

I watched the ice cream dripping from between his fingers and onto his shoes.

"I think," I said, belaboring the only point that seemed worth discussing, "that you have discovered that you really don't love me. You bought the ice cream and dragged me to this idyllic setting in order to become disengaged or unengaged or whatever."

I got up and started to walk away—slowly—and he grabbed my hand. It was a sticky handclasp, but neither of us cared. Waxing eloquent, he convinced me that he did love me, but that he was very concerned about our rushing into the engagement without God's imprimatur.

I was loath to tempt God. At this point in my Christian experience I had no assurance that God wouldn't take away what He had given. I thought it over on the bench beneath the lilacs with bees buzzing around our carton of melted ice cream; and I calculated finally that my odds would be greatly increased if I let go, if I said, "Thy will, not mine."

We prayed, and I'm sure my words were as inadequate as my motive was imperfect, but the Lord made allowance for my immaturity and my lack of graciousness. I fancied I heard Him say, "There, that wasn't so bad, was it?"

He took nothing back, and He blessed what He had given us in the first place. I recognized this when I looked up at Everett after our prayer. I wanted to tell him that I had fallen in love all over again; that this was more of a betrothal than the night he had proposed and I had accepted.

"You have ice cream on the tip of your nose," I said instead; and moistening a corner of the hanky, I gently dabbed it away.

Then we were married, and then the children came, and there were other benches and pews, other surrenders and blessings. How often I longed for still waters and green pastures, but it was not to be.

Eight-year-old Tom was stricken with polio. He had been hospitalized for a week when the call came. A woman's voice, impersonal and harsh, ordered me to the hospital. "There's been a change in your son's condition. The doctor wants you to come in right away."

She could not answer my questions: "What's wrong?" "Is he dying?" She was programed to say, "I'm sorry. I don't know. The doctor will talk to you when you get here." It was not the kind of voice to which I could say, "But I am alone with a five-year-old and a baby, and Martha isn't due home from school for a half hour, and I don't know the neighbors well enough to ask for help, and I just put my hair up in curlers, and I know this sounds crazy but I don't have a thing to wear on this unseasonably hot day in October." She would not have responded to my panic.

I phoned Everett at work. He could not be reached immediately. Was it urgent? They'd have him call me as soon as he returned. In the meantime I rehearsed my lines: "Something's wrong, Everett. They want us at the hospital right away. You'll have to go without me. There's no one to stay with the children." My speech was not quite true. I was afraid to go; I would clutch at every excuse, fabricated or real, that would justify my staying home.

The phone rang; it was Everett. I recited my lines. He said he would leave right away and call me as soon as he could. His voice was bleak.

I turned off the washing machine and carried the dripping clothes to the bathroom where I dropped them into the tub. Removing my curlers, I tied my hair back into a damp ponytail. I called my mother; she promised to come to the house right from work. Then I threw a raincoat over my housedress and waited for Martha to come home.

There were three streetcars and a bus that I had to take to get to the Contagious Disease Hospital, and it was the rush hour, crowded and slow. People seemed to be staring at me, and I touched my cheeks more than once to see if I could be crying and not know it.

Everett had arrived only a few minutes before me and was sitting on a bench across from the second-floor elevator.

"I thought you weren't coming," he said, pulling me down beside him.

"I had to. Where's Tom? How is he?"

Everett pointed to a room a few feet down the hall. "In there. He's having trouble breathing. A doctor's on his way here from Michael Reese to operate on his trachea."

A nurse handed us wrinkled gowns and face masks, and took us to the cubicle where Tom was lying. "You mustn't go all the way in," she warned. "Just stand in the doorway."

Her admonition was unnecessary; there was no room for us. I had expected—I don't know what—but not this frantic scene. Six or seven whitegowned figures were leaning intently over the table, strained voices issuing commands and counter commands; there was an array of tanks and bottles and tubes, and the sound of suction. Somewhere in the center of all this desperate concentration was our son, but we couldn't see him.

We returned to the bench and I prayed. Such a pathetic prayer, an agonizing prayer! "Lord, not this one, please!" I heard Him ask, "If not this one, then which? Martha, your firstborn, your pig-tailed tomboy? Debby, just recovering from surgery and months in a body cast? Jo, the baby and Martha's shadow? I had no answer. I switched from bargaining "Not this one" to "Not now, Lord," and He asked me, "When?"

Our pastor arrived and sat with us on the bench. I told him I could not join him in a prayer of relinquishment. Speaking softly, with a Scottish burr, his voice lost occasionally in the noise of traffic going by and the opening and closing of the elevator doors, he asked me a question,

"Are you willing to be made willing?"

I caught my breath, surprised by his words.

"That's all God requires of you, you know; that's all He needs—your invitation to Him to come in and take over the battle."

That much of a concession I could make. That much of a prayer I could pray.

The surgeon finally arrived. After completing the tracheotomy he came and sat beside us. "We're doing all we can," he said. "Now it's in Someone else's hands." He seemed embarrassed by his admission, fumbling for words. "If you believe in prayer—"

Everett came to his rescue. "We do," he assured him, "and we have prayed."

Relieved, the doctor left.

We were told that Tom was still unconscious and that it might be quite a while before we could see him. Everett suggested we go out for a walk. It was nearly midnight; we had been sitting on the hospital bench for almost eight hours. He unwrapped a Hershey bar that he had bought in the hospital lobby, and we shared it as we walked up and down the deserted boulevard. I realized I was at peace with myself and God. At precisely what moment I had laid down my arms, I didn't know.

It was like the tardy realization that an abscessed tooth has stopped throbbing or that a blinding headache is no longer there. Involuntarily, the words flashed through my mind: "Not my will, but thine."

When we reentered the hospital, a nurse met us at the elevator. "You may see your son for a few minutes." We donned fresh gowns and masks, and she led us to a room lined with iron lungs. There was an infant in one; a young, curlyheaded girl in another; a man our own age stared at us angrily from his respirator. In the farthest machine we saw Tom, whitefaced, his eyes fearful and bewildered. We spoke to him quietly, explaining what had been done to his throat and why; how the lung operated; why he couldn't speak. As we saw him gradually relaxing, we joshed him gently, "Look at it this way. It's a new experience." He grinned at the family joke, a slogan originated by five-year-old Debby to brace herself for everything from an unfamiliar dish to a first trip to the dentist. Before we left Tom that night, we told him, "You're going to be all right, you know." He believed us. That was not surprising; we believed it, too.

The organist ends her prelude; the carillon begins to chime. I am again where I began my reverie: the padded pew, the country church. I slip my hand into Everett's, glad to be back. The windows are open to the spring air, and the blended fragrance of lilac and apple blossoms is sweet and heady. A mourning dove, soft taupe of feather and gentle-eyed, alights on the window sill and surveys the assembly. Her mate calls plaintively from a nearby branch, and she flies off.

"O Lord, our lines are fallen unto us in pleasant places; yea, we have a goodly heritage," the minister proclaims enthusiastically. "Let us rise and praise God from whom all blessings flow!"

16

I Enjoyed You!

WE WERE RETURNING from our Christmas reunion in Quebec. To avoid a long stopover between trains in Windsor, we opted to do the final leg by Greyhound—a last-minute hectic switch. It was while sitting on the bus in the Detroit depot, attempting to cope with a hot beef dinner on a cardboard plate—Everett's interpretation of "Just get me a hot dog and a coke"—that I heard the words that have been haunting and convicting me ever since.

Two black women boarded our bus, a mother and her daughter. The younger of the two had come on board to get her mother settled, and having stowed the suitcases and packages above and around her, leaned over for a final embrace. The portly mother wrapped her arms around her daughter, kissed her, and said, "I enjoyed you, honey." The daughter, straightening up to leave, answered, "And I enjoyed you, Momma."

"I enjoyed you." My scalp prickled at the beautiful intimacy of the expression. I am accustomed to tossing off impersonal cliches at parting, like "I had a wonderful time!" or "It was awfully nice seeing you!" or "We must get together again soon!" Why, just sixteen hours ago I had said goodbye to my daughter and her family, whom I was not likely to see for another year, with a string of inadequate platitudes, when what I really should have said but didn't know how to pronounce were the words, "I enjoyed you."

We enjoyed each other in hair-down sessions in the kitchen.

We had stood in the overheated, crowded Ste. Foy terminal, our English conversation strangely alien in the babble of French that surrounded us. To ease the inevitable awkwardness that precedes parting, we talked of inconsequential things. Everett and I repeated our appreciation for the week of sumptuous dining: Martha and Debby had baked up a storm. We reminisced over the Christmas Eve supper and program at the Eglise Chretienne Evangelique, and the gracious *enchante*s as we were introduced to the Savards, the Funes, the Laforests, and the Desjardins—romantic appellations to provincials like Everett and me. We thanked the children again for the gloriously beautiful and bitterly cold tour of snow blanketed Isle d'Orleans on the morning after Christmas and for the caleche ride through old Quebec, viewed giddily through swirling snow, tucked snugly under fur rugs.

While we waited for our train, we rehashed things that had been said and said again. I wanted to slice through this repetitive circle of conversation to say, "I enjoyed your wonderful hospitality, but I enjoyed you more."

True, the elaborate meals were a treat for Everett and me, for we have begun to lean heavily on hamburger helpers and take-out chicken dinners; but better than the gourmet cooking were the hair-down sessions as we cleared the table and did the dishes, and the men took care of the children in the living room.

Isle d'Orleans I would not have missed for the world; I used up a roll of film on the snow-shrouded graveyards along the St. Lawrence, Everett informs me; but my happiest memory of that day is that of sitting uncomfortably in the back of the VW van, unable to see out of the steamed-up windows, with one of the twins—what difference whether it was Nate or Ben?—sleep-heavy in my lap.

And as thrilling as the caleche ride was, I enjoyed far more the morning that Martha took Debby and me on a shopping excursion, bravely asking directions of the mono-lingual bus driver, understood and understanding, getting us there and back successfully, arms full of cheeses and water colors, and the right change in our purses.

The fellowship on Christmas Eve with the French Christians was a once-in-a-lifetime experience for Everett; but he could not have enjoyed it any more than I enjoyed the late night vigil that Debby and I kept, alternating ginger ale and antacid tablets, waiting for the twenty-four-hour flu to have done with us and planning in those quiet hours the writing of this book.

"I enjoyed you, and all the short, short moments with you, and I left without telling you so. I promise myself that next time we will cut down on the sightseeing and concentrate on the companionship; and we will say goodbye from the heart."

* * *

"I enjoyed you." For a year I have not been able to put those words out of mind. It was inevitable that I should find in them a spiritual profundity. Hardly a day has passed since that time in Detroit that the Lord has not asked me, "Well, how about it? Are you enjoying Me?" Weak and human, with a more-than-average propensity for hedging, I reply, "I love Thy kingdom, Lord, and the house of Thine abode—"

"You know that's not what I mean," He chides. "Are you enjoying Me?"

"I enjoy reading the pundits," I plead. "C. S. Lewis and Francis Schaeffer. A person can't do much better than that."

"You're evading the question," He accuses. "Are you enjoy- Me?"

I try circumlocution. "I'm only truly comfortable when I'm in the company of your people, Lord; my record collection is almost exclusively Christan artists; my radios are locked in to WMBI in Chicago and WRVM in Door County, so that I hear the finest of gospel music and the cream of the conference circuit; there are scriptural mottos on my walls and hymnals on the music rack; and two young orphans in Korea who call me momma—"

"Be still," He commands. "Stop your idle babbling and know that I am God, that I am here, that I am accessible."

"To enjoy?"

"To enjoy. I am so close you can hear My footsteps; they're only a pace ahead. So close you can reach out for My hand; it's at your side. So close you can whisper, and I will answer."

"Lord, I forget."

"You're too busy watching the scenery."

"I'll cut down on the sightseeing," I promise. "I'll concentrate on the companionship."

"You won't be sorry," He assures me. "In My company there is fullness of joy, and at My right hand there are pleasures forevermore."